Idioms, Proverbs, and Sayings...

Oh my!

A humorous and educational trek through sayings you've never cared about.

Volume 1

Other books by Brad Myers:

Paid to Poop

A Humorous Look at Work and How to Avoid It

(Available on amazon.com but I don't recommend. It's pretty raunchy and not very funny.)

Other work by Brad Myers:

Enjoy my blog here: http://paidtopoop.blogspot.com/

(Meh. I don't update it, but there are some posts and all my Christmas newsletters some people find funny.)

Idioms, Proverbs, and Sayings... Oh my!

By Brad Myers

Copyright © 2024 by Brad Myers. All rights reserved.

jibcarrib@gmail.com

https://paidtopoop.blogspot.com/

All Rights Reserved. No part of this publication may be reproduced, distributed, or transmitted in any form or by any means, including photocopying, recording, or other electronic or mechanical methods, without the prior written permission of the author.

First Edition, Volume 1, 2024

Editing credit: Laurie Em; thanks for your edits! <Any mistakes are purely on me>

ISBN-13: 978-0-9855918-2-3 (Brad\Myers)

"…It'll all come out in the wash."

Acknowledgements

I wouldn't have finished this book if not for Gwen. Her support, direction, humor, heart, and <cough> unmentionables have been driving forces for me. She's made my life truly enjoyable and I've always felt loved. I hope I've done at least that for her. I do love you.

For my three sons… They never read my first book and I don't expect them to read this far into this one either. They have made being a father enjoyable and exciting. Adult potty-trained children are way more fun than poopy little children. You've all three given me more laughs than I probably deserve and I'm so thankful for you in my life.

For Grandma; she gave me my first life motto… I was 5-7 years old whining about a broken toy or something so incredibly important to a 5-7 year old that I don't even remember what it was. Heck, it could have been a brother or sister calling me a name, I just don't remember. But I do remember her picking me up off the floor relieving me from my tantrum and straightening me up. She hugged me.

She then stepped back, placed her hands on my shoulders and looked lovingly in my eyes like a cartoon animal. Support like this was hard to come by. Years later I'd reflect back and hoped that young parents today would handle their kids/grandkids in the same manner…

"Stop your whining, it'll all come out in the wash. Now go home."

Idioms

    Proverbs

        And

            Sayings…

Oh my!

Have you ever heard someone say something nonsensical and wondered what the heck they were talking about? Well, you're about to get a book full of that. Maybe you heard someone make a connection between apples and healthcare. Or maybe you didn't know whether you should or should not shake a lamb's tail, or how many times it should be shaken. (Answer: Zero times). But what if I told you they were right?

What if an apple a day increases your intake of vitamin C and phenols (antioxidants) which promote better digestion, thus making you healthier, with potentially fewer doctor visits? Apples may be linked to the prevention of Alzheimer's disease. Is that nonsensical? Whoa!

What about cats in bags, brown noses, throwing of babies, and the extremely popular question; do all good things come in small packages? These are all idioms, proverbs, or sayings and I'll let you know in two shakes of a lamb's tail what those are by definition.

But first, please read on after the definitions as I take you through some sayings you may be familiar with and some you are not. You might learn things you never cared to know, and you might repeat things you aren't sure are true. However, at this point, I already have your money. The research is real. The content is solid. The humor is subjective.

I have taken about 80 sayings and given the explanation, the history, and some example usage. I then add my own comedic take on what these different idioms, proverbs, and sayings mean to me or what they make me think of when I hear them.

Here are the definitions of idiom, proverb, and saying from dictionary.com:

Idiom:
(noun) - An expression whose meaning is not predictable from the usual meanings of its constituent elements, as *kick the bucket* or *hang one's head*, or from the general grammatical rules of a language, as *the table round* for *the round table*, and that is not a constituent of a larger expression of like characteristics. A language, dialect, or style of speaking peculiar to a people.

Proverb:
(noun) – A saying referring to common fact, knowledge.

Saying:
(noun) – Something said, especially a proverb or apothegm.

What is an "apothegm"? Hold on, I'll go check… … Ok, I found it:

Apothegm:
(noun) - A short, pithy, instructive saying; a terse remark or aphorism.

Oh, for Pete's sake! What is an "aphorism"? Be right back, this is ridiculous…

Aphorism:
(noun) A terse saying embodying a general truth, or astute observation, as *"Power tends to corrupt, and absolute power corrupts absolutely."*

They used big words to describe other words. Except that last one; 'sayings'? Why did they make that more difficult? Sheesh, let's look at them this way:

Idioms are statements about life or lessons said or shared.

Proverbs are often biblical and colorful ways to give advice.

Sayings are things that are said and perhaps carry significant enough meaning to be repeated by others, 'sayings' is often used when referring to idioms and/or proverbs.

That was a pain. But I guess it's also an example of me going above and beyond to give you accurate information. Sure, I just looked it up on dictionary.com but at least you didn't have to. You're welcome.

Idioms, proverbs, and sayings, we have all heard them and even repeated them, but do we really know what they mean or where they came from? Probably not, we typically don't care. We just say things we've heard and repeat them without really knowing the true meaning or history behind them. Maybe knowing the meaning won't change how you use a particular saying, but perhaps you'll gain a better understanding of the history behind the sayings you use and it will help you win trivia contests and get you in, or out of, more bar fights. You might even get smarter!

As a young boy growing up in the Pacific Northwest, I learned many of these sayings from overly-repeated conversations from overly-drunk Elks club members during weekend campouts. I was also exposed to relentless repetition from my father's mouth in many a situation where he would drop some knowledge on a salesclerk.

As a matter of fact, I'll ease you in to one of my favorite sayings, with a true short story. This particular saying happens to be rooted in the Pacific Northwest. Nonetheless, it's a saying my Dad would repeat many times in his life, and each time I was embarrassed because I didn't know what it meant; turns out he didn't either… And we certainly didn't know the history.

Sunlight sliced through Pacific Northwest pine trees, warming my face, while a slow, cool breeze tussled my late 1970's feathered locks. Dusk in early September cast long shadows and was always my favorite time of day. It was mostly calm and comfortable, and the perfect time for a walk to the store.

Just through the woods and past a neighborhood sat a little 7-11 convenience store. My friend, Jeff, and I walked this path many times in our youth- mostly on the evenings of a sleepover. We would loiter the 7-11 and fill our sacks with cheap candy, comic books, sports cards, and lots of memories.

We'd practice Kung-Fu on young Alder trees and pioneer a sport which would later be called "Parkour" on unsuspecting Juniper bushes. Some nights we would even tip some empty milk crate towers behind the Thriftway. But it was the 7-11 that was always the destination, and this particular evening was no more or less special than any other. Except for the fact that I was about to do something I'd catch myself doing for many more years to come.

I stalked the candy aisle (I'm actually not sure if 7-11 ever sold anything but candy. Actually, not true, because later in life I found a huge fondness for their nachos and that gooey cheese, Big Gulps and Slurpees). I stuffed my sack with penny candy, a Big Hunk bar, Zots, Sixlets, a 7-Up candy bar, and a 3-Musketeers for my Dad.

I put my two dollars on the counter and tried to glance over the clerk's shoulder at the Playboy and Penthouse magazines on the back rack; I was eleven years old and intrigued. The clerk had long stringy hair and a tie-dyed Grateful Dead shirt, and his breath reeked like skunk. As he slid the 3-Musketeers bar into the sack, I recalled something my Dad would say in situations like this, so I repeated it:

Me: *"We all should have been born rich instead of good looking. That way we wouldn't have to work for a living."*

The clerk shrugged and curled his lips in a smile and handed me my change;

Clerk: *"Ha ha... gnarly, dude."*

Ugh. I literally threw up a bit in my mouth just typing that. My Dad said that all the time and here I was, just eleven years old, and saying it to a twenty-year-old hippy! What had I become? I started repeating things he always said to people, even though I thought it was stupid, old, or just 'dad-like.' It was the defining moment for years to come that I would continue to repeat these stupid things and never find a cure.

I put the change in my pocket, grabbed my sack and looked for Jeff to get out of there. I found him at the comic book rack flipping pages and wheezing a little bit- he had bad asthma.

Me: *"Come on, let's go."*

Jeff: *"Hold on, I've got maple bar on my fingers and this comic. Got a hanky?"*

Jeff always had an affinity for stopping at the bakery next to the Thriftway and buying day old baked goods. If we didn't walk behind the Thriftway and vandalize the stacks of milk crates, we would walk in front of it which was a small strip of stores, one of which was a bakery. Jeff would stop in and buy day old donuts on the cheap. I'm not sure why I thought that was odd, but the fact was he always had a lot of food for very little money- it was weird to look across the Sorry! board at Jeff sitting there with an entire cake on the table and a piece of pie in his hand.

I went over to the hot dog roller and grabbed a handful of napkins and gave them to Jeff. He wiped his fingers a bit, licked 'em, then dabbed the back of the magazine but only made it worse. So, he just crammed the comic book between two others, glanced around and scurried out behind me.

We walked and chewed in silence for a little bit, past the strip mall and back into the neighborhood. As my mouth and teeth wrestled with my Big Hunk bar, I started thinking back to just before we left the house because I wasn't sure if my Dad was drunk when he gave me the money or if he really meant what he said. I replayed the conversation in my head...

Jeff and I had been playing Monopoly when we decided to go to the store. I needed some money for candy, maybe get some Junior Mints and Whoppers and then come back home for a Risk and Life marathon. But I needed money – and my dad had it. Borrowing from him always came at a price. I understood it was his money, but I was in grade school and earned $1.00 every two weeks for allowance and never had enough to even pay attention. Sometimes he let me off easy with a short, direct response:

Me: *"Dad, can I borrow a couple bucks so Jeff and I can go to the store?"*

Dad: *"No."*

Still, other times he made it more elaborate and included his own request:

Me: *"Daddy, may I have an advance on my allowance so Jeff and I can go get ourselves a treat?"*

Dad: *"No, and can you get me another Buckhorn outta the fridge? Thanks."*

But of course, there were the times, like this one, where he would include his own lecture of some kind:

Me: *"Father, would it be ok if I borrowed a couple of dollars today and you can keep my allowance for the next month?"*

Dad: *"You know, son, I'm going to give you those dollars and a little something more: Advice. Now you're not going to get this from any book, but what I'm about to tell you and your friend ..."Jeff", is it? I'm going to help you not be taken advantage of in the future. It'll make you smarter...Maybe not Jeff over there, but you never can tell."*

He got out of his Lazy Boy, pulled out his wallet and fetched a couple of singles and strolled over to where Jeff and I stood in fear. He folded them in one hand and grasped my shoulders in that "fatherly-advice" sort of way. His hands were rough, worn, and strong like an old vice. Jeff inched backwards toward the door.

Dad let out a disappointed sigh before he spoke. I turned my head a little to my left to make sure Jeff wasn't sneaking out but also to avoid Dad's breath which stunk of cigarettes and bad beer. And then he said it…

"Don't take any wooden nickels."

My dad said some stupid shit when I was growing up, but this one trumped all others before it. "Wooden nickels"? What the hell is a wooden nickel? He must have thought I was a complete idiot, not wrong, but he must have also thought that what he said would mean something to me.

I took the two dollars, thanked him, then Jeff and I backed out the door. Neither of us mentioned what had happened because we had no idea what it meant. I thought my dad just made that stuff up on the fly. I certainly never questioned it. It was my dad, it had to be true. Dads were the Internet of my generation: If he said it, it must be a real thing.

I put the rest of the Big Hunk back in the sack. I waited a few seconds for Jeff to stop chewing so I could ask him what he thought…

Me: "*Hey Jeff, whattya think my dad meant by that, 'don't take wooden money' thing?*"

Jeff: "*I dunno, was he drunk again?*"

Me: "*Sure, but am I supposed to learn something from it? …You've got pie on your cheek.*"

Jeff: "*Maybe.*" He said, moving pie from face to sleeve. "*Do you ever learn when he says shit like that?*"

Me: "*Guess not…He told me not to hang out with you.*"

We walked through the neighborhood and Parkoured the forest, got back to my house and into my room where we dumped our sack of goods. I had all the candy I wanted and was sorting it out while Jeff sat there with his sack of old doughnuts and pie on his sleeve. I just pointed at his arm, laughed and called him a pig. Jeff was punching me when my Dad burst into my bedroom.

Dad: "*Hey, you're back, did you get me anything?*"

Me: *"Yeah, here's your 3-Musketeers!"*

Dad: *"Great, thanks. Where's my change?"*

Me: *"Oh, here you go."*

I stood up and dug around in my pocket and placed the contents in his palm. He looked down at the change, scowled and said,

Dad: *"What the hell, son? You owe me fifteen cents!"*

He haphazardly tossed three coins onto the Monopoly board, and incredibly, they landed on Free Parking.

Dad: *"I told you not to take any wooden nickels!"*

He stormed out. Jeff picked up the coins as I bent to see what they were. That hippy clerk stuck me with wooden money! I couldn't believe I fell for it. Actually, it made perfect sense because I was pretty stupid. Jeff lit up with laughter at my expense. I turned to punch him but he raised his hands and gasped, and day-old donut spittle splattered my face. He laughed so hard and long that he became useless for five minutes.

I wiped my face on Jeff's jacket and sat down and started counting my Monopoly money---which is also fake… And no, I didn't notice that irony until right now.

I never looked up what, *"Don't take any wooden nickels"* meant back then. But I have now and you can fast forward to that later in the book. For now, just be sure to never accept fake money unless you're playing Monopoly.

Those were fun days as a kid-- with all the sleepovers, candy bars, board games, and being verbally abused. I had a good childhood, and my Dad taught me valuable lessons, like how to properly hold a .38 Special revolver and to avoid the business end at all costs—a lesson he would purposely fail many years later and die from self-induced lead poisoning.

Because of that, it prompted me to question the things he taught me over the years. What else have I learned from his teachings or things he repeated so often? What have I retained and passed on to my children and is any of that even valid? I needed to find out.

My initial research for this book quickly revealed that my Dad and the Internet are both full of shit sometimes. My Dad either made stuff up on the fly or stole stuff from the likes of Andy Capp and Beetle Bailey, and maybe a little Hägar the Horrible.

However, it turns out that there is actually much more to the idioms and sayings you know and use today. Some are heaped in history and tradition. Others are from famous authors and playwrights. Religion plays a significant role in many of the phrases and proverbs that sometimes add color and style to our lives—much like board games and candy bars did for mine.

My Dad was a smart and funny man, and some of the things he said have annoyed, embarrassed, and even hurt me. But he taught me a lot through his repetition. The research I have done has been incredibly rewarding for me and I hope you find it informative and funny. I think my Dad would have loved this book, or he would have said he did anyway.

The sayings I chose to put in this version were meaningful to me in some way or another. Some I hadn't heard before, so I was interested to learn. Your favorite may not be here and I'm sorry about that, but drop me an email and I'll try and get it in the next version. Ohhhh, foreshadowing alert!

Please enjoy:

Absence Makes the Heart Grow Fonder

Explanation:

Your feelings for something or someone can increase given time apart. Time spent away might help you place more value in that thing or person.

History:

Some poet named Francis Davison wrote one of the modern translations in his *"Poetical Rhapsody"* in 1602. However, THE William Shakespeare in 1604 during *"Othello"* wrote;

"I dote upon his very absence."

But we have to go back even further, like before year 1, to find the earliest form of this saying. Sometime before 15 BC; Sextus Propertius wrote it in one of the four books of his *"Elegies"*:

"Always toward absent lovers loves tide stronger flows."

Reads like gibberish to me but lots of takeaways for the reader on this one:

- I'll be giving you many ways to win bar trivia night throughout this book.
- Be careful though, you'll get beat up more times than you'll win bar trivia night for spouting off your knowledge of poets.
- Become a poet for all the awesome tail you'll get, just don't brag about it. You'll be more attractive to others, but won't be appreciated until after you're dead.
- Name one of your children "Sextus." They'll thank you later.

Example:

> **Dad Of The Year:** *"It's ok, Charlie. We're sending Fluffy to live on a farm for a year so she can run free and do dog things. Since absence makes the heart grow fonder, your love for Fluffy will grow and grow! And just remember when Fluffy sees you after a whole year, her heart will have grown*

fonder too! ... Assuming she survives the harsh winter and the coyotes and bears."

Charlie: *"<Sniff>"*

Brad says:

(*Absence Makes the Heart Grow Fonder*)

- I'm not so sure in all cases. Consider the absence of good heart health; neglecting your heart can help your heart die faster.
- Even when that absent person is someone you hate, your heart grows fonder the longer they stay away.
- Sometimes it's not the absence of the person that your heart grows fonder for, it's the fact that you can't remember what they look like. Then, when you do finally get to see them, you're like, *"OH Yeah! Now I remember... Meh."*
- Except in the case of incompetent Managers/Bosses/Directors. They never had the ability for their heart to grow fonder. Our only hope is that cardiomegaly eventually resolves their condition.
- Except in the case of my dead pet... Absence makes my heart grow sadder.

Actions Speak Louder Than Words

Explanation:

What you do is usually more important, or has more impact, than what you say. Doing something makes a bigger statement than just talking about doing it. How you act around your children and how you treat other people teaches them more than what you say to them.

History:

Biblical. 1 John 3:18:

> "...Little children, let us not love in word or talk but in deed and in truth."

Pretty boring, right? Well, check this out because it has certainly been said and written many times over the years. Most noteworthy might be when Abraham Lincoln said it in 1860 during his famous speech. Nope, not the speech about Gettysburg, either.

Sorry, but it was his Cooper Union Address that elevated his national awareness as he elaborated his views on slavery:

> "...Here, then, we have twenty-three out of our thirty-nine fathers "who framed the government under which we live," who have, upon their official responsibility and their corporal oaths, acted upon the very question which the text affirms they "understood just as well, and even better than we do now;" and twenty-one of them - a clear majority of the whole "thirty-nine" - so acting upon it as to make them guilty of gross political impropriety and willful perjury, if, in their understanding, any proper division between local and federal authority, or anything in the Constitution they had made themselves, and sworn to support, forbade the Federal Government to control as to slavery in the federal territories. Thus the twenty-one acted; and, as actions speak louder than words, so actions, under such responsibility, speak still louder..."

He had not yet announced that he was going to run for President at the time of this address, and many say the Cooper Union Address could be responsible for making him President.

Abraham Lincoln said many words, and gave eloquent speeches, but it was his follow through and actions that spoke the loudest and eventually helped save a nation.

Example:

>**Older Brother:** *"I was telling her to donate money to the Salvation Army bucket at Christmas time. But then I realized actions speak louder than words, so I thrust her hand in to the bucket and made her let go of her money."*
>
>**Mother:** *"I think the 'action' you were needing to take was to put your own money in to show your sister?"*
>
>**Older Brother:** *"I need a bike. Besides, I did show her, she just took more than she left. She's a little thief! Whattya want for Christmas, Ma?"*
>
>**Mother:** *"Better children. Might start working on that tonight."*
>
>**Older Brother:** *"Hey, we're good chil... Wait, what? GROSS!"*

Or,

>**Friend On The Phone With Dude:** *"Dude, I told Shelley she was pretty but she didn't seem to believe me."*
>
>**Dude On The Phone With Friend:** *"That's very sweet, but you should know that actions speak louder than words; take*

some flowers down to her work, make her a mixtape, and cook her a nice meal… Like I just did for her last night!

Shelley In Dude's Bed: *"Dude, can you make me breakfast?"*

Brad says:

(*Actions Speak Louder Than Words*)

- Public farting is an action that can be muffled by loud words. Say loud words while farting and nobody will know it's you. Unless the words you say loudly are, *"Hey everybody, I'm farting!"*
- Giving flowers in lieu of an apology is an action that speaks louder than words (also, you don't have to actually say those words so you're really not sorry and win every argument). And yes, I'm single now.
- Punching someone in the lips means more than just saying to someone like, *"Ohhh, I'm gonna sock you in the puss!"* However, if you can say that while you are punching someone in the lips then that's just kick-ass!
- Be warned! If you do something like tell people you donate money to help cure cancer and then DO NOT donate that money, your non-action obviously speaks louder than words. However, if you never get caught, you'll still have the recognition and admiration of your friends… and cancer. You're definitely getting cancer if you do something like that. Donate, don't tell.

Adding Insult to Injury

Explanation:

If you're '*adding insult to injury*' you're not solving any problem, you're actually making the situation even worse than it already is. For example, you might be accused of adding insult to injury when you point out that someone's car insurance is going to go up because they just got another ticket. That person is still pissed about the money for the ticket- you just added '*insult to injury*' by pointing out something they hadn't thought of.

History:

I could find only one historical mention of this phrase: playwright Edward Moore in 1748 used it in his play *"The Foundling."* The text from the play is a bit tough to swallow, much like reading my dribble, but here it is from page 191 (all sic):

> *"(To Sir Roger) Bel. No matter, Fidelia – Well, Sir! – You have been robb'd, you say?"*
>
> *"(To Villiard) Vill. And will have Justice, Sir. Bel. Take it from this Hand then. (Drawing) Sir Chu. Hold, Sir! – This is adding Insult to Injuies..."*

I have no idea what I just read, hoping you understand it. Seems there are no references to being 'injured' physically. I guess you could be in a car accident and your wife smashed her face all up and you could say, *"Gee, you're ugly now. Bye."* That's an insult to the injury. I'm still single.

Example:

> **Whiny High School Footballer:** *"Not only did we lose the game, but now we're also out of the playoffs... Talk about adding insult to injury!"*

Or,

Mother To Her Friend: *"She failed the final with an F+ ... What's the '+' for? Whatever... Since she failed health class, she doesn't get to drive all summer. Oh and adding insult to injury; Blacklung Community College won't accept her now with that failing grade."*

Brad says:

(*Adding Insult to Injury*)

- One of my favorite warehouse stories – what? You don't have a favorite warehouse story? – Three of us were throwing 3" X 3" cardboard squares at each other over the lumber stacks. One day, this dude peeked around a stack and another dude hit him right in the eye socket with one of those corners. He went down in a heap of tears and whining. Hilarious! The dude who hit him with the corner ran to the office to get first aid and to let the uppers know what happened. When he returned with some bandages, he just tossed them down next to his crumpled form and said, *"Since you're just lying around on the job, I went ahead and punched your time card out for you."* Adding insult to injury on the job!
- This can work backwards, too…I was riding my bicycle with a buddy and he said to me, *"You're too fat for that bicycle."* Right after that, my front tire fell off and I went over the handlebars and scraped my face on the pavement. That's adding *injury* to an *insult*. Well played, buddy!
- You can tell someone, *"Hey, I was going to get you a birthday gift but I really don't like your face, it's crooked. So instead, take this…"* Then punch them right in the lips—you just added injury to an insult, which is different, but it's because you think "outside the box". Reward = 1 beer.

- Sometimes it's a veiled compliment that makes the insult almost seem like a compliment. Let's say you twisted your ankle and it started to swell. I might walk by and say, *"Wow, that fat ankle makes your legs look skinnier."* I just added an insult with a compliment to your injury because I think outside the box too, and I'm a jackass.

All Is Fair In Love and War

Explanation:

This proverb means that anything goes when it comes to love and war. In war, there are no rules to achieve your directive. The same is true in love, in that you should follow your heart and not be burdened by rules (other than the actual laws, you sicko. No means no!).

History:

From Don Quixote, 1620:

"Love and warre are all one: and as in warre it is lauful to use sleights and strategms to overcome the enemy. So in amorous strifes and competencies, impostures and juggling tricks are held for good, to attaine to the wished end."

Then, in 1717, playwright William Taverner wrote the following in, *"The Artful Husband"*

"All advantages are fair in Love and War."

But it was in 1789 when the current form was written in, *"The Relapse, or Myrtle Bank"* multiple contributors:

"Tho' this was a confounded lie, my friend, 'all is fair in love and war'..."

Example:

Dad: *"Did you really steal your girl from your best friend?"*

Son: *"Yeah, all is fair in love and war."*

Dad: *"Truth! That's how you were made."*

Or,

Billy: *"I want to see Cindy so bad."*

Teddy: *"Why? What are you waiting for? Call her and head on over."*

Billy: *"She's out with Larry."*

Teddy: *"Oh, then go show up on their date, make a scene, get your woman! Remember, all is fair in love and war."*

Billy: *"They're at a strip club."*

Teddy: *"I'm going with you."*

Brad says:

(*All Is Fair In Love and War*)

- Seems aggressive to say you can do in love what you can do in war. Love and war are diametrically opposed. Although the card game, War, was pretty cool. You'd each place a card face up at the same time and if they were the same card, you'd say, "War!" Then you'd each play three cards face down, called a "Threesome," and then you would… Hey, now I get the 'love to war' reference. Those 18th century folks got their freak on!
- In war you're sometimes trying to conquer other countries. In love you're sometimes trying to conquer other countries without the 'o'.
- All is fair in love and war seems like another one of those excuses to lie and cheat. A way to justify your wrong-doings. It's like when someone starts a statement with, "*No offense, …*" They are really just about to offend you. But if someone just stole your significant other and said, "*All is fair in love and war.*" Then they are both douchebags.

- It would be nice if we could love and not war.

All Thumbs

Explanation:

"All thumbs" means you are very awkward or clumsy, particularly with your hands. If someone has told you, *"You're all thumbs!"* you've probably made a mess of things. In response, just put all of your thumbs up and leave the mess for them.

History:

Another John Haywood Collection of 1546:

"When he should get aught, each finger is a thumb."

Dang, now I need to look up "aught." Hold on…Sorry that took so long, but I guess it means "anything at all." Still doesn't make it clear for me. Hopefully you're smarter.

Example:

Al: *"No, I can't play the piano, I've been told I'm all thumbs."*

Al's Best Friend: *"No, you were told you have no piano talent."*

Or,

Trent: *"I tried knitting and sewing, but I just don't have the dexterity, I think I'm all thumbs. I think I'll try coloring."*

Trent's Thumbs: *"Thank goodness! Crayons are softer than needles, right?"*

Brad says:

(*All Thumbs*)

- *"Whoa, dude, you have ALL thumbs! That's amazing!"*
- Useful when hitchhiking, but also confusing: *"Thank you ALL for stopping."*
- Great for hanging black light posters in your bedroom with thumbtacks, bad for picking your nose.
- I think the saddest thing about being all thumbs is not being able to do that "here's the church, here's the steeple, open the doors and look at all the people" thing. It'd just be a church full of stubby little uglies in there.
- If you were all thumbs it would make pointing at something remarkably difficult and, well, pointless (haha, get it?). It'd just be stubby thumbs pointing in different directions. You'd have to point using your whole fist.
- I think all thumbs on your feet instead of toes would be remarkably beneficial. You could climb better, pick things up with proficiency, and otherwise just be a real fun topic of conversation at the beach or Podiatrist office.
- Embarrassing! Every time I'm mad at someone and flip them the bird, they just think I'm giving them a thumbs up. Which I am!!! Ugh, damn thumbs.

An Apple a Day Keeps the Doctor Away

Explanation:

It literally means that if you add an apple a day to your diet, the health benefits will help keep you and the doctor from having to meet as often. Rich in vitamin C and phenols, all varieties of apples will help your immune system, cholesterol, and even some research shows it can help protect against Alzheimer's disease. Told ya.

History:

The nutritional value in an apple is thought to be enough to keep you from getting sick and having to go to the doctor. But this is actually a phrase that became popular in the late 1800's, credited first to *"Notes and Queries"* magazine which had this:

> *"A Pembrokeshire proverb. Eat an apple on going to bed, and you'll keep the doctor from earning his bread."*

Mean to doctors, for sure, because they need to eat too. But it was the turn of the 20th century that it started to circulate a little more in its well-known form, "An apple a day, keeps the doctor away."

Example:

You: "I've been eating fruits and vegetables and feel better than I ever have. I haven't been to the doctor in over a year!"

Me: "Do you eat apples?"

You: "Yes I do. It's a fruit."

Me: "An apple a day keeps the doctor away."

You: "You're an idiot."

Brad says:

(*An Apple a Day Keeps the Doctor Away*)

- A cheeseburger a day keeps the skinny away.
- A gun in his face, keeps the doctor in place.
- If you eat 3 apples a day, you'll crap all week.
- Nobody seems to care about the doctor. They need human interaction and friends too. We should be considerate of everyone. So, eat your apple, but also take up smoking cigarettes to help even the playing field so doctors get to see you once in a while.
- Does eating apple Jolly Ranchers count? If so, I'll never see a doctor.

The Apple Doesn't Fall Far From the Tree

Explanation:

Typically used to describe children being much like their parents in appearance and personality. Children might have a very similar personality or make the same life choices in relationships and careers as their parents did before them. Sometimes it's a compliment but can be used derogatively as when a parent and child are 'rotten apples.'

History:

Could be a German proverb from 1842, or even Ralph Waldo Emerson in 1839. But the Germans attribute it to the Turks who then say it was Russian in origin. Lest we not forget that in 1605 or 1585 Megiserus < Who?> also lists it as Turkish, originally. It would seem to me that everyone had their mitts on this one. I guess apple trees and children and good/bad parents exist on all continents.

Example:

> **Beth to Her Friend:** *"Your daughter is beautiful! With her golden, curly hair and those dimples, she is a mirror image of you! I guess it's true, the apple doesn't fall far from the tree."*

Or,

> **Frank, An Awkwardly Proud Bad Man:** *"My son's in jail again. This time he took his friends car and ran it into a convenience store, robbed the clerk and took off on foot."*
>
> **Parole Board:** *"Frank, this is your parole hearing, we don't need to hear how your son is repeating your mistakes."*

An Awkwardly Proud Bad Man: *"I'm not going anywhere. I'm just preparing you to meet my son. The apple doesn't fall far from the tree now does it?"*

Brad says:

(The Apple Doesn't Fall Far From the Tree)

- Apples won't fall far from a tree, unless that tree is in orbit-- around Earth—'cause then those apples are going to fall forever ... In orbit! Get it?!?!" Like, falling at 17k miles per hour! Ahahahahhaa. Science jokes are funny.
- I think it really depends on which tree you are using in comparison. I mean it certainly fell far from that tree *WAY* over there.
- Who says the apple fell? Perhaps the Earth rushed up. It's all relative. Boo-yeah, two science jokes!
- Some apples fall because they deserve it, like rotten apples. The same is true with people. Rotten people seem to breed and raise rotten people. But that's not necessarily true either, might just be circumstance. I'm really all over the place. Apples make me hungry for pie. I bet rotten apples would be good in pie, much like rotten bananas are high in sugar content and good in banana bread. Remember that movie, "*American Pie*?" I wanna try that now.
- More proof of apples not falling far from the tree; Sir Isaac Newton. That dude took an apple on the noggin' and will swear he wasn't far from the tree. Science joke count: 3
- Sometimes you hope the apples fall so far from the tree that they never behave or act like that tree – in certain situations or mannerisms. Like when Dad used to 'turbo-fart.' He'd rattle off 7-9 farts in half as many seconds while giving us all 'finger-guns." I'm an apple that fell far from that tree.
- Too many people in my immediate circle share a similar trait in their patriarchal tree in the way they met their demise. I

hope all of the apples fall so far from that type of tree in this sense, that they never stop rolling.

An Albatross around His Neck

Explanation:

"An albatross around your neck" is a symbol of something bad you have done or that keeps causing you grief. It's symbolic of some burden you must carry. Carrying a large dead bird around your neck is cumbersome and something you certainly don't need or want!

History:

From Samuel Taylor Coleridge's, *"The Rime of the Ancient Mariner"* in 1798 where a man kills an albatross and is forced to wear it around his neck as a reminder of his cruelty.

...
At length did cross an Albatross,
Thorough the fog it came;
As if it had been a Christian soul,
We hailed it in God's name.
...
'God save thee, ancient Mariner!
From the fiends, that plague thee thus!—
Why look'st thou so?'—With my cross-bow
I shot the ALBATROSS.
...
And I had done a hellish thing,
And it would work 'em woe:
For all averred, I had killed the bird
That made the breeze to blow.
Ah wretch! said they, the bird to slay,
That made the breeze to blow!
...
Ah! well a-day! what evil looks
Had I from old and young!
Instead of the cross, the Albatross
About my neck was hung.
...

Example:

Disgruntled Boat Owner (DBO): *"My boat breaks down every year costing thousands of dollars but I still love it. But it's become an albatross around my neck, and I don't know what to do."*

Friend of DBO: *"Sink it."*

DBO: *"I need different friends."*

Or,

Bad Choice Bob: *"I didn't pay taxes for a couple of years and it's caught up to me. The government is now garnishing* *my wages – It's like an albatross around my neck for the next 5 years!"*

Brad says:

(*An Albatross Around His Neck*)

- "Hey guys, I feel really bad about killing that bird, but is there any chance I could wear a dead parakeet or anything with a smaller wing span? It's starting to molt."
- "Listen, I forgive you for telling me I had a fat shadow. Now will you take that dead bird off your neck?"
- "Yo, check out my new neck bling, bruh!"
- In "*The Rime of the Ancient Mariner*" the dude killed a bird and then had to wear it around his neck to remind him of his cruelty. Yet, isn't that equally cruel if your perspective is from other flying albatrosses? Albotrossi, Albotri? Those birds have to witness that and how do you think that makes them feel? Point is, that's a big bird, alive or dead. The one around your neck might smell pretty bad but a living, flying, 10 pound poop machine with vengeance in its tiny heart is what you should be worried about. Poops away!
- If you had to wear what you killed as a punishment in today's world I think 'murdering's' would be slightly less.

All That Glitters Is Not Gold
Don't Judge A Book by Its Cover
Looks Can Be Deceiving

Explanation:

I've lumped these three sayings together because I'm inherently lazy, but also because they are similar. When you hear any of these three, you can think;

What may look good on the outside may be bad on the inside. And the reverse could also be true; what may look bad on the outside may be good on the inside.

History:

Looks can be deceiving – I didn't find any relevant information on where or when this came from. Pass.

Don't judge a book by its cover – This idiom was first recorded in June 1867 in the newspaper Piqua Democrat:

"Don't judge a book by its cover, see a man by his cloth, as there is often a good deal of solid worth and superior skill underneath a jacket and yaller pants."

All that glitters is not gold - Good research will reveal that the word "glitters" is a mispronunciation of the actual word, "glisters," used in Shakespeare's play, *The Merchant of Venice*, 1596. That's what good research will tell you, but you're reading this, so maybe don't admit you know that. Unless it's under one of two circumstances:

1. Trivia night. Or,
2. If it will get you out of a bar fight. But my guess is; if you're spittin' Shakespeare quotes at a bar somewhere, you're already in a fight. Best to shut up.

Even better research may reveal that various forms of this same saying were common before Shakespeare. However, unless you want absolutely nobody talking to you at parties; don't tell them that it was Alain de Lille who in the 12th century wrote,

"*Do not hold everything gold that shines like gold.*"

And certainly don't reveal your new found knowledge that Geoffrey Chaucer's, *The House of Fame,* in 1380 stated;

"*Hit is not al gold, that glareth.*"

Like a python! Look at that knowledge I just dropped. Remember the movie, *Good Will Hunting*, 1997? Matt Damon was a super smart guy (suspension of disbelief, please) and in one scene at a local bar he schools a smartass dude who just regurgitated book smarts. Smack down! Don't be that smartass. Be sure to see *Good Will Hunting*, and then take your knowledge of who really first stated "*all that glitters is not gold*" and deliver a knowledge bump to their head! Boom! Also; hands up, protect your face and ears, duck and run!

Example:

- All that glitters is not gold means that just because something is shiny, does not mean it's valuable.
    - Like all the makeup you might put on your face to hide the fact that you're kind of ugly.
- Judging a book by its cover means you are making assumptions about something based only on what you can see on the outside.
    - In the literal reference of using a book, you actually do this every time you look at the cover of a book. Typically, that's the only information you might have regarding the book so you make a judgment right there about the book, based on its cover.

- - In a literal human reference: When I wear Under Armor brand underwear and nothing else. I know the only thing "Under" that shirt is far from "Armor" it's just hiding many years of fat and shame. But you don't know that part! You look at me and think, "Sick!" (Both Urban and Webster dictionary meanings apply).
- Looks can be deceiving sums up the other two in that sometimes pretty things are horrible and sometimes ugly things are wonderful.
  - Pretty things that are horrible: Just check out dolphins and ducks and polar bears in your Googles. They are adorable but are utterly horrible creatures. Go check, I'll wait for you to return ... Here's a search to get you started: *"pretty animals that are horrible"*
  - Ugly things that are wonderful: Look up vultures, manta ray, or naked mole rat! Careful searching on that last one, you might get more hits in areas you didn't want. These are examples of things that look terrible, but are harmless. Unlike the hippopotamus which is both ugly and mean, think mother-in-law, D'OH! Geez! Question: Is an incredibly easy, tired, and lame joke worth leaving here for you to sigh at me? Yes, word count baby! Also, my mother-in-law is a beautiful person inside and out.
  - Someone selling you a used automobile might have painted it, cleaned the interior, and even put an air freshener in there. Looks can be deceiving! Once you look under the hood, you find that the motor is a hamster with 3 legs and a rectangular running wheel. That won't work! Don't buy it. And please give that hamster a better home (or at least a round wheel).
  - Humans. We are both remarkably pretty, ugly, horrible, and wonderful often at the same time. Just always be wonderful.

Brad says:

(All That Glitters Is Not Gold / Don't Judge A Book by Its Cover/ Looks Can Be Deceiving)

- Looks can be deceiving because Tanya Harding was a pretty thing but was a horrible person. While Roseanne Barr was an ugly thing who was wonderfully funny. Now, before passing judgment on me for my judgment of Roseanne, I was talking about her character. Go see why she was kicked off of her own show in 2018 and you'll see the ugly underneath.
- Your towns' Mayor and hobos are often judged by their appearances. Your Mayor may be well dressed and appear to be an upstanding person. Your hobo may be less-well dressed and appear to be a deviant. Sometimes, they are the same person. But when a hobo glitters, it could be because he was just partying with a stripper. But when a mayor glitters, it's definitely because he was partying with a stripper.
- All that glitters is not gold: Some necklaces. Some earrings. Some teeth.
- All gold glitters.
- Certainly you judged this book by its cover. Actually, it was only purchased by family and friends so you judged it by obligation…Soooo… Thank you!

Another Day, another Dollar

Explanation:

Not necessarily literal, unless you're remarkably underpaid. If someone says, "Another day, another dollar" they are referring to their work day as just another work day and pay in the humdrum life that is work. Whoa. That's deep and sad. You might say this when asked about your work day to avoid discussing anything about work.

History:

And now you're gonna get your $1's worth: This appears to just be a saying with no historical trail that I can find and I'm not going to dig any deeper because I've literally worked a day on this and made less than a dollar on this book you're reading.

Example:

A Guy Who Doesn't Like Tommy Anymore: *"After spending all day stacking boxes, Tommy knocked them all down. So tomorrow, we have to start all over again. But whattya gonna do? Another day, another dollar, I guess."*

Or,

Mary Ann: *"How was your day?"*

Me: *"Well, I read a thousand sayings, edited hundreds of them, felt delusional and stupid beyond any help, and otherwise disgusted with my lack of talent. Oh, the good news is that I worked on "Another day, another dollar" today so I can already complete my taxes for next year. Income = $1.00 US. 'Cause my mom'll buy it!"*
(I just wrote "mom'll")

Brad says:

(*Another Day, another Dollar*)

- Sure, if you're lucky enough to make a dollar a day. My allowance was $1 a week and I was lucky to get that.
- "Another day, another dollar?" I can't tell if you're bragging or complaining!
- In some parts of the world a dollar a day is probably a lot of money. Of course, that dollar can only be used for goods and services here in America, so those people are screwed. And in America, I think we are getting rid of the dollar or at least trying real hard to – I don't have any dollars. We might even get rid of all the dollars.
- Sometimes it's another day but the same dollar. And other times it's the same day and a different dollar which would make it two dollars on that same day. Work for that.
- I know what my retirement job is going to be-- Oh, sorry, an explanation is needed here. A retirement job is the job you have to take after retiring from the job you just lost to a younger less expensive summbitch. So, I'm going to be a cashier at one of those Dollar stores where everything costs a dollar. And as I swipe each and every item I'm going to say, "*Another day, another dollar*" and drop it in the sack. I'll just make full eye contact with the purchaser, swipe the trinket, beach ball or can of 6 month expired chili, and say, "*Another day, another dollar.*" <drop>. I'll keep doing it until I get punched in the face by a rival retiree or raped in the back lot in the back lot.
- If you ask someone about their work day and they drop this gem on you, "*Another day, another dollar.*" You should really care less about their day and more

about yours. Better still, ask to borrow that dollar and never talk to them again.

Barking Up the Wrong Tree

Explanation:

This phrase describes a mistake you or someone else might have made in judgment; either on accident or on purpose. Dogs will sometimes tree a squirrel and stand at the base barking up the tree. However, the squirrel may very well have jumped to the next tree and moved along. If you've falsely accused someone of something then you're barking up the wrong tree.

History:

This phrase is credited to James Kirke Paulding in his work, "*Westward Ho!*" in 1832. However (and this is important), initial research will point you to "*Westward Ho!*" by Charles Kingsley and Malcom day, dated 1835.

Do we have a feud here?

What you've just experienced is me digging a little deeper to get you the truth. I don't always try hard, but when I do dig for more information, it better be right where I was looking. Why would I work this hard for you? Because I care about how you'll use information in this book. Trivia night at the bar? You got it. Fighting over who said what? You're empowered now. So the next time you're arguing with someone about the age of exploration and who wrote "*Westward Ho!*," you tell them two things:

1) You tell them it was actually James Kirke Paulding's work that this phrase is credited to a full 2 years before Kingsley grabbed it, and…

2) You defend your honor with, "*You're barking up the wrong tree, bubba*!"

Example:

An example might be in a childhood game of "Hide-and-Seek" where you might send someone "barking up the wrong tree" by telling them to check the garage—while you know everyone is in the back yard.

Or,

< The majestic pirate stood in front of me, his flowing blonde hair flicking about his face, giving me small glimpses of his steely eyes. He pressed me against the bulkhead and demanded my surrender. As captain of my own vessel, I addressed the situation thusly, >

Me: *"You're barking up the wrong tree, fella. The Captain is over there."* I lied, pointing to my friend, Pegleg Paul.

<The pirate and his men then killed Pegleg Paul and all the rest of my men. He then made me his slave and I had to wash his feet at night and pick stuff out of his beard after dinner. I guess I barked up the wrong tree, too. Gotta go, my turn in the barrel!>

Brad says:

(*Barking Up the Wrong Tree*)

➢ I've been beaten up in High School for barking up the wrong skirt.
➢ Super bad waste of time if you've barked up the wrong tree, because you still have to bark up the right tree. Assuming you can find the right tree, you may never be sure. Sometimes barking is just a bunch of noise.

- I send Jehovah's Witnesses barking up the wrong tree when I tell them to go talk to my atheist neighbors, George and Tom, they've been happily married for 12 years and don't like any people.

- So I guess a quiet dog at the base of a tree means it's the right tree? But if you can't see the dog and you can't hear the dog, then you'd have no idea what tree. So then you'd tell the dog, "*Bark, boy, so I know where you are!*" Then the dog would be barking at the base of the tree. Now, is it the right tree or is he barking up the wrong tree? You don't know! Dog marks tree. Stupid humans.

- Maybe when a dog finds the right tree they just stand upright and nod toward the tree as if to say, "*This is the right tree, feed me.*" Smart dogs!

Beat around the Bush / Beat about the Bush

Explanation:

This phrase refers to someone who is not necessarily getting... Well, it's like when they want to say something but just keep getting lost. They might get close to explaining something but... Gosh, it's like trying to explain a phrase or saying but not really coming out and just stating what it means. So, someone who is beating around the bush isn't, or rather doesn't stop explaining what it is they are trying to explain. It's like Tetris – stuff keeps falling and you're working to put the pieces (words) in the right place to make your point(s), but you just never finish.

Someone who is 'beating around the bush' is not getting to the point of their conversation quickly.

History:

Officially it appears in a mediaeval poem around 1440, *Generydes – A Romance in Seven-line Stanzas*:

> "Butt as it hath be sayde full long agoo,
> Some bete the bussh and some the byrdes take."

Those aren't typos, that's how poets wrote while they sipped ale and waited for the Knights to return from killing dragons.

George Gascoigne's, *Works*, in 1572 said it more clearly:

> "He bet about the bush, whyles other caught the birds."

Again, not a typo but it reads better. However, what you're really interested in is how this phrase came about. Well, bird hunters in England would hire people to scare birds from the bush by going in there and causing a ruckus. When the birds fled, hunters took aim and shot, thus killing the previously sleeping birds. This wasn't the safest line of work because it wasn't always just birds they might flush out. Sleeping bears, mountain cats, wild boars, frazzled hobos – it was always a risk.

So the workers started beating the bush with sticks rather than going in and risking themselves. This wasn't as effective as diving right in so hunters would accuse them of beating around the bush and encourage them to dive in the bush and flush the critters out.

Example:

> < Your son is doodling on a sheet of paper next to his math workbook; he's clearly not doing his homework >
>
> **You:** *"Son, stop beating around the bush and get your homework done."*
>
> Or…
>
> **Man:** *"Darling, will you…Would you please…Hmmm. Honey, I love you and want to spend…A lot of time with you. I've given this a lot of thought and would like to ask you to … to…"*
>
> **Woman:** *"Stop beating around the bush and just ask me!!!"*
>
> **Man:** *"OK, I'd like to ask you to stop nagging me about getting married!"*

Brad says:

> (*Beat Around the Bush*)
>
> ➤ Did we really need to hire people to make noise in the foliage back then? Did yelling not work? Couldn't a hunter throw rocks or sticks into the bush? I'm all for employing people but it seems this process could have been automated.
>
> ➤ If I paid someone to beat the bush and they simply beat around the bush, I'd take issue with that. I don't know what the hiring laws were back then but it sounds like they were

just lazy kids. Fire 'em and find some better employees. Kids those days, am I right?

➤ On the other side, if I were the person paid to go in and beat the bush and it became dangerous for me, I might choose to beat around the bush as well. Realizing the consequences of my actions back in those days, I'd at least try to fake it better. Maybe I'd muffle my voice like I'm in the bush, throw out a couple of, *"Ouch, stickers!"* Things like that to make it real. Later I'd be cleaning their horses and picking up dung all day.

➤ An awkward teenage boy might do this while experiencing his first woman.

The Bee's Knees

Explanation:

A phrase that describes something as "the best" or extraordinary. Synonyms over the years would be 'decent', 'excellent', 'cool', 'awesome', 'fire', and my favorite, 'on fleek.' Might even refer to actual bee's knees where they carry pollen which ultimately produces delicious, sweet, honey.

History:

Props to the American flappers of the 1920's for popularizing this term. But actual credit for origin would have to go to Mrs. Townley Ward who in 1797 wrote, "*It cannot be as big as a bee's knee.*" However, that connection to 'things that are small' was lost and you've already got dancing flappers on your mind (Google that!).

The initial meaning of bees knees referred to something that was meaningless. Like telling someone they need a left handed toothbrush or having someone check your viscosity switch on your Ford Model T (that last one is a joke because the viscosity switch wasn't introduced until 1927 with Ford's Model A). But in the "Roaring 20's" the dancing flappers turned it into a term of excellence that was used for many years until the 1950/60's brought in 'cool.' But 'cool' wasn't cool, until The Fonz made it "cool."

Example:

> **Questionable Morals Carol:** *"Everyone's wearing knickers, Charlene, why they're the bee's knees this year! Scott Thomas said he liked my hair today. Scott is so dreamy, he's just so athletic and handsome! I might let him into my knickers this evening."*
>
> **Charlene:** *"Wow, Carol, you sound like Scott is the bee's knees, not your knickers."*
>
> **Questionable Morals Carol:** *"He is! And if he's nice he might just get "beeee-tween these knees" tomorrow night!"*
>
> **Charlene:** *"Gross, thanks for ruining bees for me."*

Brad says:

(*The Bee's Knees*)

- *"Gee Sammy, your dancing is spectacular, you're the bee's knees!"*
  "I guess that's better than being the bull's balls."
- Why the bee's knees? Because the bee's knees are the tastiest part of the bee.
- Bees are our friends and remarkably cute. Wasps, hornets, not so much. Bees are the bee's knees ….Wasps are Worst and Hornets Horrible.
- There's really not much to say about this one. It's a nonsense expression and really nothing funny about it and it shouldn't even be used any more… So STOP IT!

Beggars Can't Be Choosers
Don't Look a Gift Horse in the Mouth

Explanation:

I'm going to save trees by combining these two proverbs as they are similar in meaning and history. So, the rest of this is going to read pretty awkwardly as I navigate two at a time. Working without a net here to give you and the environment the best deal. If you're not used to my awkwardness by now – well, you've already stopped reading a while ago so you're not affected. However, if you're still reading and annoyed AND you didn't buy this book, you're looking a gift horse in the mouth because you're annoyed by something that was given to you.

Beggars can't be choosers:
- This proverb teaches that if you asked for something, and it is given, then you shouldn't question the value/quantity/quality of what you were given.

Don't look a gift horse in the mouth:

- You shouldn't criticize a free thing.
- Don't be critical of gifts you receive. Just take it, feign happy, smile, and say, *"Thank you."* You can always throw it away or re-gift it later.
- Don't question the quality of a free gift or express dissatisfaction.
- Don't assess the gift and wish for more.
- If someone says to you, *"Don't look a gift horse in the mouth,"* you've probably been ungrateful or disrespectful regarding the gift.

History:

  Both of these proverbs have roughly the same origin: John Heywood in the 16th century. His long titled book *A dialogue conteinying the nomber in effect of all the prouerbes in the Englishe tongue* was later reduced to *"The Proverbs of John Heywood."* This book was just a list of sayings he heard and jotted down, but he is credited with many sayings.

  I wonder if he wrote this because so many people said it to him after he jotted down what they just said without even buying them an ale. However, it is likely that he got *"don't look a gift horse in the mouth"* from a Latin phrase from *"The Letter to the Ephesians,"* written by St. Jerome in 400ish which was, *"Never inspect the teeth of a given horse."*

  That's a boring history, I was hoping for something about a guy looking a horse in the mouth and having his nose and eyes bit off. That's a better reason not to look *any* horse in the mouth.

  Horses used to be incredibly valuable when they were used to plow fields, to transport people and goods, or otherwise to haul and help lift heavy items. It was good practice to check the health of a horse you were planning to purchase. A horse's mouth and jaw may show signs of abuse or overwork if the person didn't take care of their animals. However, it was bad manners to thoroughly examine a horse that was given for free.

Example:

Beggars can't be choosers:

>**Beggar:** *"Hey, can I have a blanket?"*
>
>**Person With Blankets:** *"Sure, here you go…"*
>
>**Beggar:** *"Oh, thanks, ummm, not the grey one, maybe the…No…Do you have blue? I guess I'll take the…"*
>
>**Person With Blankets:** *"BEGGARS CAN'T BE CHOOSERS!!!"*

Don't look a gift horse in the mouth:

>**Clint:** *"Hey Chuck, you gave me this free rake, but it's super old, smells funny, and I think this is poop on the handle. Smell."*
>
>**Chuck:** *"It was free, Clint! Sheesh, don't look a gift horse in the mouth."*
>
>**Clint:** *"Oh? You have a horse, too?"*

Or,

>**Sandy:** *"I know the drapes are not the right color, Sally. But don't look a gift horse in the mouth. Your mother worked hard on those and they were free!"*

Sally: *"You're right. I should be more grateful. By the way, do you want the blouse you gave me? It's too big and ugly for me."*

Brad says:

(*Beggars Can't Be Choosers / Don't Look A Gift Horse in the Mouth*)

- Why can't a beggar be a chooser?
  "Here you are, beggar, I found this half eaten peach wrapped up in some dirty underwear under that dead guy over there, you looked hungry."
  "Um, no thank you." Good chooser!
- Beggars can be choosers, when they choose to beg.
- Beggars are choosers when they choose to do something about their plight and make a cardboard sign and ask you for money on the street. You've seen 'em. You usually choose to look away. They're still there.
- How many people get horses for gifts? I must be the worst gift-giver ever!
- "Don't look a gift horse in the mouth" is the old fashioned way to tell your children, *"Have better manners and appreciation for what you are given."*
- I might get you a gift card or a re-gift of a vegetable slicer but if I ever give you a horse, there's something seriously wrong with our relationship.
- I think it's perfectly acceptable to look a gift horse in the mouth. I want to know why you're dumping this nearly dead animal on me. Why would you unload a perfectly good horse? Open wide, friend.
- Always look a gift horse in the heart. Someone thinks you're pretty special to give you an entire horse. The horse is special too. Name him/her Ed or Edwina.

The Best Things in Life Are Free

Explanation:

Some of the most gratifying, happiest, and satisfying events in life won't cost any money. Spending time with family and friends, taking a neighborhood walk, hiking the trails are just a few examples. The connection is that the best things in life are things like love, companionship, relationships, your friends and family and that these things do not take money to create or nurture.

History:

Credited to the 1927 musical, *"Good News"*, this proverb was in the song titled, <wait for it...> "The Best Things in Life are Free."

*"The best things in life are free
Now that I've discovered
What you mean to me..."*

Example:

Husband: *"We spent the entire weekend just playing with the kids and working on cleaning the yard. It was my favorite weekend."*

Wife: *"The best things in life are free."*

Husband: *"No, no, I had to pay the kids $4 an hour to play and work, but totally worth it!"*

Wife: *"So, the best things in life are $4?"*

Brad says:

(*The Best Things in Life Are Free*)
- ➢ Not this book.

- Not even a 'gift horse' apparently.
- Porn can be free. There is a TON of free porn on the Internet, so I've heard, but you can't browse it at the library.
- Like taking your children to Disneyland, sure the trip costs money but the best things about the trip are the memories and those didn't cost anything…Except $5000.00 and a week of your life you will never get back.
- Nothing is free—except maybe your last breath. You're not going to have to pay for that.
- Giving compliments. Giving them is free, feeling them is wonderful.

Between Two Stools

Explanation:

This describes a difficult situation because you need to choose between two different choices. It could mean you haven't decided on which choice to make putting you 'between two stools.' It can also refer to a situation where you've failed to make either choice in time and failed on both choices. This puts you between the two stools rather than sitting on one of them. The stools represent a couple of difficult decisions to make so you are between two decisions.

History:

This phrase was first written in the poem "Confessio Amantis" in 1390 by John Gower:

> "Bot it is seid and evere shal,
> Between tuo stoles lyth the fal
> Whan that men wenen best to sitte."

Example:

Blake: *"In state college or out of state, Dad, I just can't decide."*

Steve: *"Son, it's your decision, and a big one. I'm afraid you're between two stools."*

Blake: *"Huh?"*

Steve: *"You have to choose one or the other."*

Or,

Beverly: *"I think you're between two stools on this one, Sandy."*

Sandy: *"Why?"*

Beverly: *"Because Jim and Steve both left and found other girls. You didn't choose and they moved on, now you don't have anyone."*

Sandy: *"I still have you."*

Beverly: *"Nope."*

Brad says:

(Between Two Stools)

- Between two stools means that the current time must be between 6:15AM and 6:45AM for me. Yes, I'm that regular.
- The implication was that if you didn't choose one stool or the other, you would end up sitting between them and fall to the ground. Which is actually a good perspective to make a difficult decision. You've fallen and learned and can now see the two choices from a different perspective, both literally and figuratively. Nothing funny, just a lesson that failing to choose can sometimes lead to better things.
- Choosing between two stools can be difficult in and of itself. Sometimes the stool at the end of the bar is better than the second one in since you have easier access to the bathroom. But you also want the one that faces a window… Or maybe the one that faces the rest of the bar so you can people watch. Careful though, that stool at the end is most often next to Cliff Clavin.
- You can pick your friends and you can pick your stool, but you can't pick your friend's stool.

Birds of a Feather Flock Together
A Man Is Known By the Company He Keeps

Explanation:

Birds live, play, migrate, and survive together in their same species. So, birds of a feather flock together might describe you and your group of friends; are you flocking with the right people? Are your friends good birds or bad birds? If your friends feed the hungry, help the homeless, and shoe the shoeless, then good flockin'! If you're nervous or scared around your friends, find better friends.

You become known by the actions (whether good or bad) by the friends you surround yourself with. Guilty by association.

History:

Birds of a feather flock together is a 16th century translation of Plato's *The Republic*, which was written in 360 BC. But it's Aesop's fable, *"The Ass and His Purchaser"* that inspired the proverb: "a man is known by the company he keeps."

It's about a man who wants to buy an ass and the owner says he can take the ass home for a trial; so the man did. As soon as he got this ass home to his other asses, this new ass went straight to the laziest ass in the herd and hung around that ass all day. Both of those lazy asses started chatting up the other active asses and swayed them into doing what they were doing, which was nothing! Assholes! The next day, the man had a field of lazy asses and none of them wanted to work. So the man returned this lazy ass and refused to purchase it because it was going to be just as lazy as his laziest ass. Asses of a feather flock together.

Example:

Mom: *"Brady, I don't want you hanging out with Charlie and his friends anymore."*

Brady: *"But mom, he's a good guy."*

Mom: *"No, he hangs out with Ted and Gary and those boys are in and out of jail all the time. Charlie has been making the same bad choices lately, and birds of a feather flock together. I don't want to see you follow that same path."*

Brad says:

(*Birds of a Feather Flock Together / A Man Is Known By the Company He Keeps*)

- I dunno, follow the herd. If all of your friends were to jump off a bridge, would you do it too? I say yes, because who wants to live in a world with no friends?
- Are Lemmings birds? Because they seem pretty stupid and they all hang out together, and then they all run off a cliff. Weird. Don't be a bird of this feather.
- If you surround yourself with idiots, you'll be known as an idiot. If you surround yourself with successful idiots, you'll be known as a successful idiot…But still an idiot.
- Look at the people around you right now. Are they stupid? Then you're stupid. Are they pretty? Then you're pretty. Are they angry that you keep staring at them while reading a book? Then you're creepy, stop staring!
- If your flock makes you happy and they respect you and your ability to make good choices, then stick with your flock. Regardless of what others see, you might be in the best little group of flockers you'll ever know. Hold on tight.

Black Sheep of the Family

Explanation:

A disreputable member of a family. A metaphor to describe a family member who is a disgrace.

History:

This biblical metaphor from Genesis 30:32 was about as racist as can be:

> *"Let me go through all your flocks today and remove from them every speckled or spotted sheep, every dark-colored lamb and every spotted or speckled goat. They will be my wages."*

Shepherds didn't like black sheep because their wool wasn't suitable for dying so it was worth less than white sheep.

Example:

Friend: "What is wrong with your sister? She's nothing like you and your brother- she smokes, she's mean and inconsiderate and steals. And didn't she shiv a bitch in prison? Nobody else in your family has killed someone, right?"

You: "Yeah. We think she's just misunderstood."

Friend: "Well, maybe she's the black sheep of the family."

You: "No, she's white. And she's a person."

Brad says:

(*Black Sheep of the Family*)

- ➢ It's not fair to compare a sheep and a person. Sheep are way better.
- ➢ If this were my white family and one of my sheep were black; someone would have some explaining to do.
- ➢ What is with all the hate? Even in Chess, white goes first.
- ➢ Hold on. You're saying black sheep wool wasn't suitable for dying? So to make black blankets they dyed white sheep wool, black?!? New definition of racism: Your blackness isn't as good as our ability to make white become black. I'm sick to my stomach.

Blessing in Disguise

Explanation:

This phrase is used when something is bad at first but later turns out to be quite good. A 'blessing in disguise' is when an unexpected tragedy turns out to be promising or positive in another way. Having a tree crush your house is a horrific tragedy. Having the insurance company pay to have your house roofed and sided, along with new carpet and fixtures makes that a blessing in disguise as everything is all new.

History:

Research credits English writer James Hervey with this expression in his work titled *"Reflections on a Flower Garden."* However this was written in 1746 and searching for it resulted in 28 finds for the word "blessing." But I couldn't find the reference to "blessing in disguise" specifically. Besides, that 18th century English is harder to read than something you might be currently reading. Maybe it's a blessing in disguise that I couldn't find more information because I'm going to stop writing about it now. Consider yourself, "blessed without a disguise." Moving on…

The Blind Leading the Blind

Explanation:

This biblical quote describes a situation where less informed people are leading or helping other similarly less informed people. Someone who doesn't know anything about computers might ask you to help them with their computer yet you don't know anything about computers either. You'd be the blind leading the blind.

History:

Biblical: Mathew 15:14:

> *"Let them alone: they are blind guides. And if the blind guide the blind, both shall fall into a pit."*

Wow, tough times back then! People just watched blind people walk other blind people into pits. Seems like we should have been more of a 'hands-on-helping-other-people' kind of people. Worse than that; seems there might have been a lot of pits we had to look out for back then. You don't really see many pits these days. Didn't Greece have tiger pits? Those are just awesome. I think falling into a tiger pit would be ultra-scary but also probably the most badass way to die.

Example:

Dad: *"Do you know how to paint a car?"*

Son: *"No, but Robbie watched a YouTube video on it."*

Dad: *"Does Robbie know how to paint a car?"*

Son: *"Sort of? I mean, he watched a video and everything."*

Dad: *"Son, if you don't know how and Robbie doesn't know how, you've really got the blind leading the blind here."*

Son: *"Huh? We can see just fine, I told you he WATCHED the video. Dad you dumb."*

Dad: <blink, blink> *"You're not allowed to see Robbie anymore."*

Son: *"How can we see each other if we're apparently blind?"*

Dad: <blink>, <kick>, blink>

Son: *"Fine! We aren't old enough to buy the spray cans anyway."*

Brad says:

(*The Blind Leading the Blind*)

- Stupid is as stupid does. Also, Google "I'm with stupid" shirts from the 1970's.
- If you're blind, you shouldn't be asking other blind people for directions.
- If you're blind and you're offering other blind people help on how to go somewhere, you're remarkably confident and/or horrifically mean.
- I don't even know how this happens. How does someone who's blind offer to lead other blind people?

    Blind Trying To Lead: *"Hey, over here."*

    Blind Trying To Be Lead: *"Where? ...Here?"*

Blind Trying To Lead: *"No, over HERE!"*

Blind Trying To Be Lead: *"I can't find you."*

Blind Trying To Lead: *"I'm not over there, I'm over here."*

Blind Trying To Be Lead: *"Stop moving."*

➢ If I were blind and I needed to be led somewhere, I'd have two questions and both answers have to be yes:

1. *"Can you see?"*
2. *"Have you ever led the blind before?"*

Brand Spanking New

Explanation:

This phrase is used to describe something that is completely new. A shirt that has never been worn could be called "brand spanking new." Typically used to emphasize or exaggerate the items 'newness.' Something that is just 'new' isn't as new as something 'brand spanking new.'

History:

For my purposes, we'll look at the earliest written version and that seems to be in April 1860 from *Harper's New Monthly Magazine* in an article about a sea captain (any story with a sea captain in it is badass, and you know it). The title was, "*Captain Tom: A Resurrection.*"

> "*He had a new vessel, he had a new crew, he had brand spanking new fish-gear; but he had his old luck.*"

But why "brand?" Remember that thing they did to cows with hot metal? That was a brand. Branding something secured ownership. Just like tattooing your name as a tramp stamp on your girl's trunk shelf, cowboys burned their mark in a cow's hide. A brand in marketing terms was something a business would strive to achieve.

When you pick your nose and need a place to wipe it other than the inside of your mouth, you get a Kleenex- Nobody asks for a 'facial tissue.' Kleenex is the brand. You put meatballs in a Crock-Pot, not a slow cooker, Crock-Pot is the brand. You'll ask for ChapStick before you'd ever say, "*Do you have any lip balm without hair on it?*"

- **Band-Aid** = Adhesive bandages
- **Q-Tips** = Cotton swabs.
- **Popsicle** = Registered trademark of Unilever.

- **Sharpie** = Permanent marker.
- **Tupperware** = Plastic container for your weed. Speaking of weed…
- **Weed Eater** = Motorized tool to cut tall grass. Owned by Husqvarna. Preferred term: Bush Eater.
- **Styrofoam** = Packing peanuts. Expanded polystyrene used to secure your liquor and safely package your weed for travel.

There are several more examples, Google it (ha, that's a brand right there!). So, the brand part of this phrase is referring to product recognition and if you're saying something is 'brand spanking new' then you're establishing that it is a well-known and sought after item.

Finally, we have the "spanking" part. Some sources suggest it refers to what doctors do to a new born baby- AKA "abuse." However, old English used the word to mean fast paced as Frank T Bullen did in *"The Log of a Sea-waif"*

"A large canoe…was coming off to us at a spanking rate."

Another badass sea captain setting the stage for excellent phrases! Spanking is also defined informally as 'very good'. In this case, spanking is just an intensifier helping to describe whatever you are describing. Hopefully, this book will be brand spanking new.

Example:

John: *"We got a new car. Matter of fact, it is brand spanking new!"*

Steve: *"How many miles on it?"*

John: *"One! I told you, it is brand spanking new! It's right from the factory."*

Brad says:

(Brand Spanking New)

- Babies are brand new, but as soon as you spank them, they're damaged goods. Return it.
- I might work this one into my standard method of operation when seeing or getting something new. I'll stare it down with my hands on my hips for several seconds. Then I'll just spank it and say, "*That's brand spanking new, right there.*" Then I'll spit out the side of my mouth while staring and nodding at it.
- Brand spanking new can also refer to humans, and not just babies. Remember 'the new kid' at school? That person was always exciting because they were brand spanking new. But then that same kid had a brand spanking new bike, the brand spanking new house on the corner, and even a brand spanking new Mr. Rags hooded sweatshirt. Man, I wanted to spank the brand right out of that new kid!
- I guess I actually don't understand the use of "brand" or "spanking" for that matter. The information on it is sound, but does anyone ever say this anymore? It's sort of hard to say and still sound like you're tough. For example, the two references above involved sea captains. Sea captains are badass' we know that. But the writers who wrote those stories about sea captains were not sea captains. Because no sea captain would ever say "brand spanking new."

Break a Leg

Explanation:

This is a statement of good luck said to someone who is about to go on stage. But also used in any situation you want to wish someone good luck. It was superstitious to wish an actor good luck. Counter intuitive, yes, but if you've ever dealt with actors, you'd understand. I haven't, because I know better. Actors are wonderful people, steeped in superstition! Use "break a leg" when you want to wish someone good luck.

History:

The official origin is unknown but there are many suggestions that this phrase originated in American theater in the early to mid-20th century. Actors are well known for their belief in superstition and to wish someone 'good luck' for the stage was certain doom in their minds. By wishing 'bad luck' in the form of bodily harm somehow made them feel better.

The German saying, "*Hals- und Beinbruch*" means break a leg and is possibly earlier than the English theatrical version. However, there are some interesting possibilities that have been presented as the possible source:

- If your performance was good enough, you may need to take a bow, thus bending at the knee.
- Perhaps after your excellent performance the audience might toss flowers and/or coins in excitement! You'd need to 'break your leg' to bend and pick them up.
- Just going onstage through the side curtains (known as legs) you'd be breaking the legs of the stage.
- If your performance was compared to the French actress, Sarah Bernhardt, you'd be in exemplary company. Sarah had her leg amputated in 1915 and continued to perform incredibly well.

- Or, maybe your performance killed! So did John Wilkes Booth, in the theater, in which he broke his leg when he escaped over the balcony onto the stage. Don't be like John Wilkes Booth.

Example:

Actor #1: *"My first performance, I'm SO scared!"*

Actor #2: *"Oh, you'll do fine, rehearsals were perfect."*

Actor #1: *"Crap, that's my call. I gotta go!"*

Actor #2: *"Ok, break a leg!"*

Or,

Sophomore #1: *"I'm going to bomb this test!"*

Sophomore #2: *"No way, we studied together and we're gonna ace it."*

Sophomore #1: *"Maybe."*

Sophomore #2: *"No worries, just remember what we studied and go in there and break a leg."*

Brad says:

(*Break a Leg*)

> Sometimes when I really think about it, I actually hope you do break a leg when I say, "*Hey, break a leg.*" Other times, I'm just saying it to fit in to be 'one of the guys.' But secretly, I think down deep I want everyone to break a leg, then I'll be faster than anyone. Dare to dream.

> Consider your audience. For example, you're at a wheelchair basketball game and all contestants have zero legs. It would

be rude to wish them luck with, "Break a leg." But it might be good luck to say, "Get a flat tire!"

➢ What if all professions were backward when it came to wishing good luck? For example, you might wish these people good luck in this manner:

- Fisherman – "*Hook your lip.*"
- Surgeon – "*Slash an artery.*"
- Pilot – "*Crash into a mountain.*"
- Stripper – "*Pop a boob.*"
- Engineer – "*Wreck a train.*"
- Engineer – "*Syntax to exception.*"
- Fast-food worker – "*Eat your food.*"
- Sea Captain – "*You're a bad-ass!*" Not a wish for good luck, just truth.
- Chef – "*Toss your salad.*"
- Teacher – "*Make 'em dumber.*"
- Anesthesiologist – "*Let 'em sleep.*"
- Emergency Room Doctor – "*Knock 'em dead.*"
- Lawyer – "*Hey, good luck in there and as long as we talk about the case without any direct indication of this particular case, we can't be held in contempt. Let's take it slow, think before we speak, and deliver your message slow and steady because all of this is billable hours.*"
- Librarian – "*See the movie first.*"

Bright Eyed and Bushy Tailed

Explanation:

A phrase meaning alert, excited, full of energy and ready for anything. If someone says you're "*bright eyed and bushy tailed*" it's a compliment and is usually given in the morning, after someone has awoken excited and happy for the day.

History:

The Oxford English Dictionary lists this first being printed in a song by B. Merrill in 1953,

> "*If the fox in the bush and the squirr'l in the tree be, Why in the world can't you and me be Bright eyed and bushy tailed and sparkelly as we can be.*"

Hehe, I read that like singing the song, "*Cat's in the Cradle*" by Harry Chapin and it almost works.

This reference to a squirrel is the most popular since squirrels have bushy tails and are quick, clever, and always at the ready. However, some sources say this dates to fox hunting where a fox with a listless tail, dull eyes, and slow reactions would not make for a good chase. They wanted a fox who was bright eyed and bushy tailed because it was in better health, more active, and had keen vision. Fox hunt! In either case, people ate squirrels and foxes so maybe being "lazy eyed and fat tailed" like me is a safer way to be.

Example:

Significant Other You Woke Up Next To: *"Why are you so bright eyed and bushy tailed?"*

Your Satisfied Self: *"I got up early to start my two week vacation. I was so excited I couldn't sleep!"*

Or,

Mom: *"What time do you start your new job tomorrow?"*

Daughter: *"Six AM! I'm gonna be soooo tired. Everyone is going to think I'm slow and mad."*

Mom: *"Ah, no dear, you're always bright eyed and bushy tailed in the morning, you'll be fine and they'll love you."*

Brad says:

(*Bright Eyed and Bushy Tailed*)

- ➢ What's the opposite of bright eyed and bushy tailed? Sleestak from "*Land of the Lost*" television series, 1974-1977. But they made me bright eyed and bushy tailed because they were so scary!
- ➢ Pornography web site dedicated to big eyed, untrimmed girls.

- 1970's stripper name.
- Here's to those of you who are not bright eyed and bushy tailed in the morning: May your bright eyes light up the world and you find your bushy tail and play with it all day long. Hmm, that was supposed to be cute, you know, adorbs. But it reads creepy. I was picturing a cute little fox doing it. What did you see?
- I'd like to live my life bright eyed and bushy tailed, and I've always liked people who look like they're smiling all the time – resting happy face. I'm more 'dull eyed and no tailed' all the time, but I'm happy.

Brown-Noser

Explanation:

A brown-noser is someone who acts kindly (but not necessarily sincerely) to someone else to gain their favor. Commonly used to describe a co-worker who compliments her boss for the sole purpose of getting on their good side. This person is said to have their nose so far up their boss' butt that their nose is brown. Other slang: Ass-kisser, Boot-licker.

History:

You're always looking to me for the history of these things. You say stuff like, *"You're so awesome and handsome."* Or *"You should stop writing and do stand-up, or at least do the first thing."* To that, I say, *"Stop being a brown-noser and look it up yourself, brown-noser."* Note: I didn't find a history or origin on this one, sorry.

We can guess that it was probably some disgruntled caveman who was angry at another caveman because he kept sweeping dust and dirt off of cute cavewoman's rock.

Disgruntled: *"You brush rock for one with mounds."*

Gruntled: *"Bah! So? You go kick rocks."*

Disgruntled: *"You just brown-noser."*

Gruntled: *"Huh?"*

Disgruntled: *"You keep brushing rock with nose. That why you brown-noser"*

Example:

Negative Meeting Guy: *"You know everyone calls you a brown-noser, right?"*

Positive and Bubbly Meeting Girl: "*Why? Because I have an excellent tan?*"

Negative Meeting Guy: "*No! Because every time you're in a board meeting you laugh at everything they say. And they don't say anything funny!*"

Positive and Bubbly Meeting Girl: "*Here, want my donut? Can I get you another cup of coffee?*"

Negative Meeting Guy: "*Brown-noser! ... But, yes, and yes, please.*"

Brad says:

(*Brown-noser*)

- This saying is one of those which sounds innocent but is certainly buried in grossness.
- "Boot-licker" is another term and is actually more disgusting.
- Brown-noser = Stripper name with a specific focus.
- If your nose gets brown on it, you're doing it wrong.
- Although, sometimes, if your nose gets brown on it, you're doing it right.
- "Ass-kisser" is another term for brown-noser. There is less chance of getting Hepatitis C by kissing an asscheek than there is while getting your nose brown.

Bury the Hatchet

Explanation:

To make peace. If you "bury the hatchet," you have agreed to settle your differences. Burying the hatchet with someone means you have decided to stop fighting, forget about the issue, and remain friends.

History:

The act of literally burying hatchets comes from a 17th century American Indian tradition of a peace agreement between two or more tribes. Chieftains would physically bury their hatchets in the ground together as a sign of peace and good will. The hatchet was a primary tool for survival, including chopping wood for fires, cutting hide from animals, and of course scalping your neighbors. The act of burying your most prized tool/weapon was a serious bond between tribes and people.

Today, if someone wants to bury the hatchet with you, they want to forgive and forget your differences. Moving on from troubling issues with your relationships is important for both of you to grow. However, knowing where your enemy buried their hatchet is of course exceptional intel. Get digging!

Example:

>**Fester:** *"Look, I don't like what you did and I don't like you."*
>
>**Lurch:** *"Ok, I'm sorry but let's get past this. Let's bury the hatchet and move on. Ok?"*
>
>**Fester:** *"Fine, yes. But can we bury it in Gomez' head!? I've had three in mine already today."*

Brad says:

(Bury the Hatchet)

- Did they use the hatchet to bury the hatchet? I'm guessing a shovel was pretty useful too. But if you buried the shovels, you'd need a third shovel and then it'd be awkward because one of you would have a shovel and the other wouldn't.
- An alternative to peace was to bury your own hatchet in the skull of your enemy so you'd get his land and women…And a second hatchet!
- I wonder if there were ever arguments over how deep they should bury the hatchet. If not deep enough, some kid would find it and poke his eye out or chop off a friend's finger. Too deep and I think a couple of head-dressed Indian Chieftains digging in the dirt becomes a little embarrassing for everyone. I say they should have just tapped the heads of their hatchets together three times, apologized to each other, hugged, and then sheathed their hatchets. That way there is less work and more time for Peace Pipe!

By The Skin of Your Teeth

Explanation:

This Biblical saying is used when someone barely escapes something or just completes something by the narrowest of margins.

History:

From Job 19:20:

"*…I am nothing but skin and bones; I have escaped only by the skin of my teeth…*"

Not much context from just this one line, go check it out in the bible, Job 19 "*Then Job replied.*" This chapter is Job talking to his friends about how God has wronged him. Maybe I should have included a "woe is me" saying in here somewhere. Sheesh.

Example:

Skater dude: "*Gnarly, dude! I was lucky to land that Kickflip, Indy Grab on the tip of the ramp! I would have died!*"

Skater dude's friend: "*Yeah, brah, you made that by the skin of your teeth!*"

Brad says:

(*By The Skin of Your Teeth*)

- ➢ Gross! Skin of your teeth? Then your mouth would always taste like your arm, or worse!
- ➢ That would suck if your teeth were made of skin. You couldn't eat jaw-breakers or Pez, and the only meat you could get down would be Spam—which actually is a positive. But still, your skin teeth would just mush together if you tried

biting into an apple. There's a lot wrong with having skin teeth. I don't want 'em.

- Kissing someone would be a lot like licking their fingers. This happens to be my go-to foreplay move anyway, so maybe skin teeth are just the next step towards second base!
- *"Hey buddy, you have a pimple right here, on your incisor and it's grossing me ... Oh, you popped it, gross."*
- It probably means your teeth have skin. So, your teeth are hard underneath but flesh on top. So you could get oral cancer and skin cancer at the same time.
- We'd all be tanning our teeth in the summer.
- You thought braces hurt when your teeth didn't have skin! Ouch!!!
- I don't know about all of you but I do know some of you have the same thing I do… And that's a lot of hair where we have skin. I suppose we'd be shaving and brushing our teeth.

Chew the Fat

Explanation:

Having a casual conversation. To chat or gossip in a friendly way.

History:

"Chew the cud."
"Chew the rag."
"Chew the fat."

They ate weird stuff in the late 19th century. All of these informal statements mean the same thing: to chat or idly chat to pass time. The "cud" refers to how a cow will pull up undigested food from one of their stomachs and chew it leisurely. The slow, methodic chewing represents slow chatter.

"Chew the rag" was an American military expression implying that chewing on a rag would get you nowhere but it was something to do. Idle time in the military called for patience and various ways to entertain yourself idle chatter, or "chewing the rag" would help that time pass.

"Chew the cud" was first on the scene from *The History of Tom Jones,* written by Henry Fielding in 1749:

"Having left her a little while to chew the cud, if I may use that expression, on these first tidings."

But there's not a lot of context there, better research might reveal more to satiate your appetite for knowledge on this, but I don't care. The Oxford English Dictionary references J Brunlees Patterson in his published, *Life in the Ranks of the British Army,* in 1885. He said it was a term for grumbling or complaining and that senior officers might chat with junior officers to kill time and help alleviate boredom.

It was the good old USA that coined the term "chew the rag" which would become the more modern term, "chew the fat." It simply meant idle chatter, frittering time away by chatting about anything. There are also references to Eskimos chewing whale blubber as chewing gum or stories of rich folk in the 1500's who could afford bacon would cut slabs off for guests to chew on as a sign of sharing and wealth.

Example:

Wife: "*I've had a rough day of work, I'd like to tell you about it…Care to join me for a glass of wine and just chew the fat for a bit?*"

Husband: "*Sure, honey, let me get a glass for you.*"

Or,

Heavy Set, Chubby Boyfriend: "*There you are. Hey, wanna sit around and chew the fat?*"

Husky, Plus Size Girlfriend: "*You have fat?*"

Heavy Set, Chubby Boyfriend: "*Always.*"

Brad says:

(*Chew the Fat*)

- ➢ Notice how I rambled on in the History and even repeated myself a bit? A couple of the paragraphs were disconnected, seemed like poor editing, right? Yeah, just chewin' the fat with ya up there. It didn't feel right to me either.
- ➢ If chewing the fat is like chewing on gristle, then I don't want any!
- ➢ I think next time someone wants to sit down and chat with me I'm just going to go to the refrigerator and pull out some raw

bacon or leftover steak fat and bring it back and chew on it. That way I'll be actively chewing the fat while we're chewing the fat. Multi-tasking! Actually no, that would be single-tasking but doing it twice, so twice-tasking. This conversation is tasking.

- ➤ You might go to a dinner party you weren't interested in and bring some actual fat to chew on before the party. When people want to talk, you can just tell them you already chewed the fat. Then, excuse yourself and go to the toilet and play with your phone. Spit out the fat, it's bad for you.

- ➤ If you're going to chew the fat, you should probably chew on avocados because I think that's good fat.

- ➤ Do you think that rugby team that crashed in the Andes mountains thought about the irony of what they were doing while chewing the fat? Too soon? No, because that happened in 1972 and the movie came out in 1993 and most of you reading right now weren't even born yet. See the movie or read the book- Piers Paul Read *Alive: The Story of the Andes Survivors*.

- ➤ For some conversations with my family, I'd rather chew actual fat.

Children Should Be Seen and Not Heard

Explanation:

Literally means that children should be quiet.

History:

This proverb is from "*Mirk's Festial*" which is a collection of homilies written in the 15th century by John Mirk. Here's the line from the top of page 230*:

"… for hyt ys an old Englysch sawwe: 'A mayde schuld be seen, but not herd.'"

Horribly translated: "for it is an old English saying: a maiden (young girl) should be seen, but not heard."

Example:

Scene:

Background: Obnoxious children running around playing tag. The girls are screaming and the boys are making fart sounds, yelling, "Girl germs, girl germs!"

Foreground: Two women sitting quietly, watching the commotion, one wearing a fox fur wrap and holding a goblet of wine. She tips the goblet away from her lips and says…

"*Absurd! Children should be seen and not heard.*"

Brad says:

(*Children Should Be Seen and Not Heard*)

➢ Not entirely true. Like when children are drowning in a lake and you're facing the other way talking with a friend. It would be nice to hear them so you could notify a lifeguard and continue your conversation at a louder volume and without being interrupted.

➢ Only if they are pretty children. Otherwise, children should not be seen, nor heard.

➢ However, I guess in some cases (like the first two bullets above) children should be seen AND heard, like pretty drowning children. But ugly drowning children? Pass!

➢ I like hearing children when they are adult children and say funny things. I guess I like hearing babies laugh, and young kids saying funny things from their perception of the world. Yeah, I like hearing children. All children should be heard, except when they ask for money.

Chip on Your Shoulder

Explanation:

This phrase is used to describe someone who is easily angered or becomes combative at the drop of a hat (see *Drop of a Hat, later in this book*). Someone who is said to have a chip on their shoulder is easy to upset, gets riled up quickly, and might want to fight you!

History:

"Chip" comes from chipped pieces of wood and the phrase, "chip on your shoulder" has some interesting background. One suggested origin is that it came from the 19th century in the United States as a way to challenge someone to a fight. A person would put a chip of wood on their own shoulder and dare the challenger to knock it off. Fun! But not entirely true.

In 1739, in the British Royal Navy Dockyards, Shipwrights were allowed to carry extra wood for building materials back home. They were allowed what they could carry on their shoulders and were to be inspected upon leaving. In 1753, they changed this benefit to include only what they could carry under their arm. This angered the Shipwrights and three years later, in 1756, they went on strike.

A letter from the Dockyard to the Navy Board during the strike recorded comments like;

> "*Are the chips not mine? I will not lower them.*" And, "*...Immediately the main body pushed on with their chips on their shoulders.*"

So, that's a literal history but the first figurative and written use of the current phrase is rooted in the United States in 1830 in a New York newspaper, *The Long Island Telegraph*:

> "*When two churlish boys were determined to fight, a chip would be placed on the shoulder of one, and the other demanded to knock it off at his peril.*"

Disclaimer: In my research, I did see mention of James Kirke Paulding's *Letters from the South,* in 1817, mention this quote,

> *"...This, it seems, is equivalent to throwing the glove in days of yore, or to the boyish custom of knocking a chip off the shoulder."*

However, I searched *Letters from the South* and could not find this statement. So I'm going with the 1830 history as the first *written* use.

Example:

Bender: *"Alfred sure is mad about you dating his ex-girlfriend."*

Chip: *"Yeah, he's always had a chip on his shoulder. Remember when you asked if you could date his sister and he nearly knocked your block off?"*

Or,

Beth: *"Don't ask Brenda about her recipe ingredients. She's got a chip on her shoulder about sharing anything!"*

Brad says:

(*Chip on Your Shoulder*)

- It's easy to knock a chip off someone's shoulder if you tickle them, and/or kick them in their privates first.
- I'm not sure why they'd stop British Navy dock workers from taking wood home...How else are they going to replace their disgusting teeth? That's not nice, not all British folk have bad teeth, just bad hygiene.
- I think they should bring this to Mixed Martial Arts (MMA). Two guys stand at the center of the Octagon and try to knock off pieces of wood from each other's shoulder. That would make for some hilariously boring antics.

- Was that the definition of complete toughness in the 1800's? Can you knock this piece of wood off my shoulder? Actually, I wish we'd go back to that today. Instead of shooting and stabbing each other. Kids, criminals, and cops could just settle disputes by knocking chips of wood off shoulders. Whoever remains standing with a chip of wood on their shoulder is the winner. The other person has to concede and stop doing whatever wrong they were doing. Except for cops, cops still get guns and get to tell you what to do.

- The "throwing down of the gauntlet" in medieval times was much cooler than this more recent statement. I mean, seriously, if a plate mail dude stood in front of you, took off his iron glove and threw it at your feet, you'd know you were in for some shit! But if he scrambled to find a chip of wood and awkwardly placed it on his shoulder and dared you to knock it off, you'd think it was a joke. Sure, in both cases you take a sword through your ribs, but what about respect for Knights?

- Anyone remember Robert Conrad and his Eveready battery commercials? Google that for 1970's goodness!

Close, But No Cigar

Explanation:

This means you were close to success but did not make it. Refers to falling short of making your goal(s).

History:

The first printed version of this saying is from the film script for *Annie Oakley* in 1935**, while target shooting;

> *"Get out of here!"*
> *"Close, Colonel, but no cigar."*
> *"Here you are, Bill."*

This phrase is most popular from the mid-20th century where carnival booths gave out cigars for prizes. Back in the day, if you hit the clown in the nose with the softball, you were rewarded with a carcinogen filled tube called a 'cigar.' You were better off being the clown and getting beaned in the face! If you missed the clown, you didn't win and the carny might cry out, "Close, but no cigar!"

Example:

Carl: *"Bet I can make this trash in that can over there."*

Clyde: *"That's a bet!"*

<Carl tosses the trash but it hits the rim of the can and falls to the ground.>

Clyde: *"HA! Close, but no cigar."*

Or,

Cathy: *"I really wanted to get that promotion but one of the requirements was two years of service and I'm three months away! Oh, well, close but no cigar. I'll get it next year."*

Brad says:

(*Close, But No Cigar*)

1. I almost had something really funny here. You could say I was…

Close Only Counts in Horseshoes and Hand Grenades

Explanation:

Similar to "close but no cigar" this proverb means that being less than accurate isn't good enough. There is no winning or benefit to being just 'close' to achieving something. In the game of horseshoes, tossing your literal horseshoe close to the stake does indeed score, assuming you are close enough to the stake. So, close counts in horseshoes. The hand grenade is self-explanatory as the exploding bomb will send shrapnel all over the place so you just need to be close to the target.

History:

If you look this one up, the most popular historical reference is from major league baseball's Frank Robinson in Time Magazine, July 31st, 1973

> *"Close doesn't count in baseball; close only counts in horseshoes and hand grenades."*

However, there are paywalled sources quoting this proverb as early as 1914 in a few newspapers:

> 1914 Lincoln {NE} Daily News 15 Aug.: *"Close does not {sic} count only in horseshoes."*

> 1921 Decatur {IL} Daily Review 3 Oct.: *"Close counts in horseshoes only."*

> 1932 Washington Post 8 Jul.: *"Close doesn't count except in horseshoe pitching."*

> 1970 Guthrian {Guthrie County IA} 26 Jan.: *"Close only counts in horse shoes and grenades."*

Use the baseball reference at parties. If you start citing old newspapers at your gatherings, you're gonna be invited to fewer and fewer gatherings.

Example:

> **Football Guy Familiar With Losing:** *"Don't sweat it, guys. We were close to winning and we'll do better next week."*
>
> **Football Guy Tired of Losing:** *"Close?! Close only counts in horseshoes and hand grenades!"*
>
> **Football Guy Familiar With Losing:** *"Huh?"*
>
> **Football Guy Tired of Losing:** *"We'd of won if we had hand grenades."*

Brad says:

> (*Close Only Counts In Horseshoes and Hand Grenades*)

- Horseshoes should be played with hand grenades. They took away our Lawn Darts, let's up the ante a bit!
- What if the inside of hand grenades were a bunch of tiny horseshoes? That would hurt AND be confusing.
- Wait, what if the inside of hand grenades were a bunch of tiny hands? Creepy! Like being slapped by a hundred people at once.
- I bet there are fewer fights when horses play humanshoes.
- What would you rather fight, a horse-sized duck or 100 duck-sized horses? Although, one grenade wins either fight.
- I should have looked up how horseshoes ever started... *"Hey buddy, whattya say we take that horses shoes of his hoofs and throw them at sticks? Wait, is it hoofs or hooves? I think both are acceptable. Anyway, go grab the horse, I'll untie his shoes and start throwing them at things."*

Crime Doesn't Pay

Explanation:

The saying, "crime doesn't pay" means that criminals will not benefit from illegal actions. If you steal something you will probably be caught and punished, perhaps paying restitution and/or time for your crime. Crime doesn't pay because there is a cost for every action.

History:

This saying originated as a Federal Bureau of Investigation (F.B.I.) slogan. It was first recorded in 1927 and made popular by Dick Tracy comics in 1931. I couldn't find actual use of the slogan from the FBI and I didn't search "Dick Tracy" for fear of what might show up.

Example:

Chief of Police: *"Arrests are up, fines for traffic violations have increased, and the death penalty has been reinstated. All of this as a reminder that crime doesn't pay."*

New Recruit to Senior Officer: *"I'm gonna steal that for my report."*

Or,

Your Employer: *"Stealing office supplies again and now you're fired. Son, crime doesn't pay."*

You: *"Yeah, I can see that now."*

Your Employer: *"Ok, well, go pick up your last paycheck."*

You: *"Thanks, do you know anyone who wants to buy a bunch of pens and sticky notes?"*

Your Employer: *"Check with Alan in Accounting..."*

Brad says:

(Crime Doesn't Pay)

- It pays better than whining about being poor.
- Giving hand jobs in the bar bathroom for beer money is a crime that does pay.
- If crime doesn't pay, you're doing it wrong.
- Pay isn't everything in a career package. You have to look at other stuff, too. Like, well, all the other 'stuff' you'd have from stealing it. Like notepads, coffee, paper…
- You've never heard the saying, "Crime doesn't have a good benefit program." You know why you haven't heard that? Because the benefits are fantastic, so don't focus on the pay. Now, the downside is the severance package can sometimes be EXACTLY that- they'll sever your package!
- Crime does pay when you steal money.
- It's not a crime until you get caught. So you don't need to be good at crime, just good at not being caught

Curiosity Killed the Cat

"Sorry, it's curiosity"

Explanation:

This proverb is used to explain to someone that they may be acting too curious or perhaps prying too deeply into affairs that aren't their own. Perhaps someone is being too inquisitive about your recent health exam. You might tell them that 'curiosity killed the cat' to get them to understand you don't want to tell them anything more. This is something you might say to warn others that you don't want to be disturbed.

History:

This proverb actually started as 'care killed the cat' by Ben Jonson in his 1598 play, *"Every Man in His Humour."* But 'care' in that time really meant worry, rather than to provide help for someone or something. The curiosity form came printed in *"The Galveston Daily News"* in 1898. Since cats seem completely driven by curiosity, it is believed that this will lead them all to extinction. At least, that's what all cats want us to think as they plot to take over the world. Zombie Apocalypse? Nope! That's a cat idea. It makes us worried about something else so we don't focus on them and their plans to destroy us.

Example:

Lucy: *"Did you hear about Carl losing his job?"*

Bart: *"No! What happened?"*

Lucy: *"I don't know, I'm not going to ask him."*

Bart: *"Why not?"*

Lucy: *"He can be mean and you know curiosity killed the cat, right? I don't want to ask him... But, I heard he might have actually ran over a cat with his cab."*

Carl: *"Hey, what are you guys talking about?"*

Lucy and Bart: *"Nothing."*

Brad says:

(*Curiosity Killed the Cat*)

- Technically, Kevin killed the cat when he pushed the button, not knowing that the cat was curiously rummaging through the trash compactor.
- Curiosity killed the cat, but impulse buying killed my credit.
    - Pasta and pizza killed my cholesterol.
    - Beer and candy killed my six pack. Well, I killed the six pack and then it returned the favor in the form of fat on my belly. I miss you, six pack.
    - Jobs killed my motivation.
    - Negativity kills creativity.
- "Curiosity" another good stripper name.
- It takes more than curiosity to kill a cat.
- I named my dog Curiosity because I don't like cats. I should have named him Disappointment.
- No cats were harmed in this posting, nor should they or any animal ever be! However, if I had 9 lives I'm fairly certain

I'd have spent 3-4 of those on being curious about things in my life. Like, what happens if I pee on this electric fence? Can I make this jump on my dirt bike? Will I be able to swim across this entire channel?

A Dead Ringer

Explanation:

A dead ringer is an exact duplicate of something. However, it is used more loosely in definition as closely resembling something *or* someone. If you could paint as well as Picasso, then your paintings might be considered dead ringers for his. Some stunt doubles in Hollywood are dead ringers for their celebrity counterparts because they have very similar appearance and body type.

History:

This phrase actually came from the end of the 19th century from horse racing. A "ringer" was a horse that was similar in appearance to a race horse and was used to fool bookies. The term "ringer" came to mean any duplicate of something. And "dead" in this context, means exact. Not what you were expecting? Think "dead eye," "top dead center," "dead shot," "Dead Heat" (capitals used because it's not only a real term but also a great Joe Piscopo film from 1988).

However, if that isn't a sexy enough answer for the history of a phrase, check out the following popular, goofy notion of the origin of this phrase:

In the 18th century there was a real fear of being buried alive. Even our first President of The United States of America, George Washington, had this deathbed request:

> *"Have me decently buried, but do not let my body be put into a vault in less than two days after I am dead."*

Powdered wigs and wooden teeth must have made folks crazy back then. However, the story in England was that they were running out of places to bury people so they would dig up coffins and reuse the grave. It is said that one out of 25 coffins had scratch marks on the inside. People were being buried alive!

The threat and fear of being buried alive was as real then as the fear of Martian abductions were in the 20th century. To solve this problem, they started to tie strings to the wrists of people they buried and would tie the other end to a bell at the surface. Someone would work the yard all day and night in case a 'dead ringer' needed to be 'saved by the bell'.

Plans for "Improved Burial Cases" were actually designed, built, and patented (Patent No. 81,437 Franz Vester, Newark, New Jersey – Google it). There is no evidence that I could find that these escapable coffins were actually used, but if you were looking for a business idea, there you go- send checks to Franz Vester and a bird-dog PayPal/Venmo fee to jibcarrib@gmail.com.

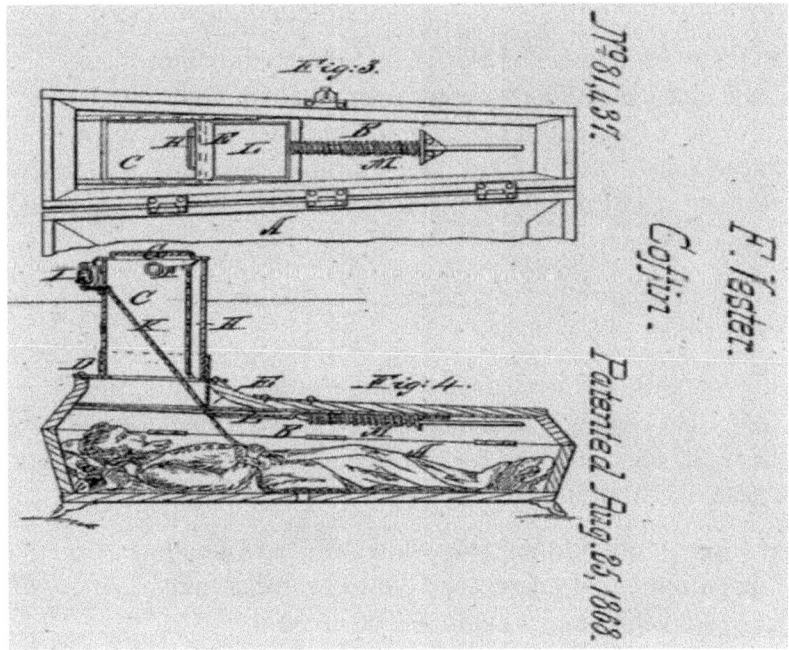

Example:

> **Store Owner:** *"Tony, these rocks you found are going to be perfect!"*
>
> **Tony:** *"Perfect for what, boss?"*

Store Owner: *"They're perfect to sell because they are dead ringers for the real Pet Rock of the 1970's and I'm going to sell a million of 'em!"*

Brad says:

(A Dead Ringer)

- This is what you should call your buddy when he proposes to his girl, gives her a ring, and she says, "Yes!" See, your buddy is a dead ringer because he's giving the ring and marriage is a type of death for singularity. I should find a day job and give up writing humor – I'm a dead ringer for the unemployment line!

- Remember "Lawn Darts?" They're banned in the United States because idiots were throwing them straight up to see how close they could get them to land near each other. A "dead ringer" was the kid lying on the ground with a red dart sticking out of the top of his head mumbling something about being a winner.

- This is a dead ringer of a sentence in this section. This is a dead ringer of a sentence in this section.

- If they really did tie strings to wrists or toes of the buried folk, I bet teenage vandals used to walk the cemeteries 'fishing' for hands and toes. You could pull one up or get resistance from the dead guy below! That would be freaky.

- If I were working the "graveyard shift" and a bell went a "dingalinging," I guarantee I didn't hear that thing. I'd just keep shoveling and whistling. Too creepy!

- It'd be just like a man to beckon for something even after he's dead.

- *"Did someone ring the dinner bell?"* Asked the pack of wolves, maggots, beetles, and grubs.

- Depending on your family life, if you were buried alive, you might just want to untie that string around your wrist and just enjoy yourself some quiet time. Nighty-night!
- I know some people on social media that would like to be buried alive with a bell and the opportunity to further dramatize their lives even after death! I say we remove the clacker.

Dig Your Own Grave

Explanation:

Someone who has dug their own grave has done something or said something foolish to put themselves in a horrible situation. If you've "dug your own grave" then you have created your own downfall based on your words and/or actions.

History:

No official history on this one. Its literal meaning might apply to when people had to actually dig their family's graves, including their own. I wonder how you decide when it's a good time to start that process? I think procrastinating is a good plan here - that way someone else is going to dig your grave for you.

Example:

>**Your Grandma:** *"If you keep cheating your friends, you'll be digging your own grave as they soon will not want to play with you any longer."*

Or,

>**Brother**: *"I did NOT read your diary. I don't even know what a diary is. Besides, if I did read it, I'm sure it was BORING!"*
>
>**Sister**: *"Liar! I found it under YOUR bed yesterday."*
>
>**Brother**: *"Boo-Hoo, why don't you go cry to your boyfriend Brad about that."*
>
>**Sister**: *"AH-HA! You just dug your own grave – My diary is the only one who knew about my crush on that hunk!"*

Brother: *"He is dreamy."*

Brad says:

(*Dig Your Own Grave*)

- ➢ Remember "adding insult to injury"? It applies here as well… I mean, you just died; then you were dropped in the hole you dug for yourself.
- ➢ I did try digging my own grave once. I got tired half way through and quit. My little brother fit in there just fine, though. It's his now.
- ➢ I was also arrested in a cemetery once for digging my own grave. The cop said, *"Son, you're digging your own grave by digging your own grave."*
- ➢ I think I'll dig my own grave in my neighbor's yard, her lawn is nicer than mine.
- ➢ That would be weird to have a heart attack while digging your own grave. You'd fall in, someone would rescue you and take you to the hospital. You'd survive, live a great life and then die and be placed in your grave again. Worst déjà vu ever!

Doesn't Have a Leg to Stand On

Explanation:

This is used to represent a lack of support for an argument or position. To "*not have a leg to stand on*" would mean you are in a situation where you cannot prove anything. Legs support the body like evidence supports a case. Without evidence you don't have the support to fight/argue the case.

History:

I could not find any historical evidence for this saying. I'm going to guess that it occurred in the old west. Let's say a drunk cowboy was accused of stealing goats and when confronted he was wobbly and could barely stand. The Sheriff said, "*Boy, I know you stole those goats, but you're so drunk and guilty, you won't have a leg to stand on.*"

Whomever said this first probably made it up and didn't have a leg to stand on when asked what it meant. I know I won't have a leg to stand on if I start digging up history and then make stuff up so I'm going to stop now.

Example:

Cop: "*Did you see her steal the soap.*"

Store clerk: "*I didn't actually see her take the soap.*"

Cop: "*Then you won't have a leg to stand on if you accuse her.*"

Or,

Peg Leg Pam: "*You're cheating on me!*"

Poor Taste Paul: "*I am not and I would never do that!*"

Peg Leg Pam: "*I saw you with her yesterday in the park and again at the pub.*"

Poor Taste Paul: "*That's simply not true. I was at work all day, you can ask Pat.*"

Peg Leg Pam: "*Nope, nope, nope, it was you.*"

Poor Taste Paul: "*I'm sick of these accusations, you're always doing this and you don't have a...*"

Peg Leg Pam: "*A what, Paul? I don't have a WHAT?*"

Poor Taste Paul: "<gulp>"

Brad says:

(*Doesn't Have a Leg to Stand On*)

- It's not nice to simply point out people's ailments.
- He DOES have another leg to stand on, and I've seen a lot of people with only one leg get along just fine. We have to think positively no matter how many legs we have or don't have.
- It should really be, "*They don't have a foot to stand on*" because that's what we stand on. The leg is just a buffer between our butt cheek and ankle. With no leg, we'd call them bunkles instead of cankles.
- Pirate captains get along with one leg to stand on and they've probably fibbed their whole life. Sure not all pirate captains have only one leg, but certainly the ones with the best stories to tell only have one leg… And one eye. Who's more likely to tell you the truth, the guy with two healthy legs able to scamper away on a whim? Or the guy with one leg made from a oak branch with no depth perception? Trust the pirate captain, he has less to lose, literally.

Don't Take Any Wooden Nickels

Explanation:
Don't let yourself be cheated out of something. Don't trade something valuable for something that has no value.

History:
In Washington State, around 1931-33, when a bank failed, round wooden coins were issued to fill the shortage of money. You would be able to exchange them later when non-wooden money became available. The wooden coins had an expiration date and sometimes a specific redemption time. You didn't want to be holding any wooden nickels when they became useless. Now it's just a way of saying, "don't get scammed by anyone."

Example:

> **Mama:** *"Now, darling, when you head into town and sell that saddle, I don't want you to take any wooden nickels."*
>
> **Daughter:** *"Wooden nickels, mama?"*
>
> **Mama:** *"Sorry, honey. Yes, don't be like Brad and let those city folk fool you with fake money or something you don't need. Take cold hard cash only!"*

Brad says:

(*Don't Take Any Wooden Nickels*)

- Leave it to the Pacific Northwest tree huggers to take their number one natural resource and turn it into currency rather than cutting it down and selling it for real money.
- You know who cares the most if your money is made from old growth fir? Strippers. They want singles in the form of paper because wooden currency splinters and chafes.

- Sometimes it's ok to take wooden nickels as long as you get to give something in return; like a kick to the junk.
- If you need to be told not to take money made of wood, then you probably have bigger problems. However, you're not the dumbest: What about the guy making wooden nickels? If you're gonna pound wood into money, why not make them quarters or more? Also, what's a nickel? Change and paper money are nearly dead!

Don't Throw the Baby Out With the Bathwater

Explanation:

This proverb warns you to not discard something of value along with something of little or no value.

History:

This German proverb originated from Thomas Murner's satire *"Narrenbeschwörung"* (Appeal to Fools) in 1512. Sebastian Franck published a book in 1541, *"Spruchwörter"* where he used the example of sending an old horse to the knacker but forgot to take off the expensive saddle first. But that history (although true) sucks. Read this…

You may have heard the story where medieval men and boys bathed in the bathtub first, followed by women and girls. When they were done, babies were then washed in the same water. By then, the water was so murky and dark that it was possible to make a mistake and toss the baby out with the bathwater.

That may be poppycock and probably never happened but more intriguing and certainly possible given everybody was cruel and terrible in medieval times. Babies are whiny and crying all the time, I can see this happening back then.

However, worse things are happening to babies now! Being tossed out in your family's bathwater may not be such a bad plight given what goes on nowadays. Boy, this is getting dark, huh? Oh! See that? "Dark" times, like medieval period? That's pretty good. Poor babies.

Example:

Lance: *"My car is junk! I'm taking it to the junkyard and starting over. I'll just buy a new one."*

Steve: *"Take your stereo and those race seats out first, those are worth a lot of money. Don't throw the baby out with the bathwater!"*

Or,

Good Baker: *"There's a spider in this box of donuts, I'm throwing the whole thing out!"*

Bad Baker: *"Hey, hey, don't throw the baby out with the bathwater, I'll get a different box and we can still sell them."*

Brad says:

(Don't Throw The Baby Out With The Bath Water)

- …Said the bathing baby.
- Unless it's a really bad baby.
- We all make choices; sometimes it's the baby, sometimes it's the bathwater. But NEVER throw the baby out WITH the bathwater, that's wasteful.
- Have you ever tried to fish a slick baby out of a wet, somewhat soapy, bath tub? It's ridiculous! Sometimes it's easier to just throw it all out and start over.
- Babies can be annoying and letting one just slide out the end of the tub as you empty it into the river could be a common mistake. Sometimes you have to go back to the village and just say, *"Oops. Sorry 'bout that."*

Drop of a Hat

Explanation:

This phrase is used to express sudden and instant action. If someone does something "at the drop of a hat" it means they did it without hesitation or preparation.

History:

The earliest printed reference is in 1837 in the Register of Debates in Congress,

> *"They could agree in the twinkling of an eye, at the drop of a hat, at the crook of a finger, to usurp the sovereign power; they cannot agree, in four months, to relinquish it."*

I'm not sure of the actual origin as it stands to reason it was around and in use long before 1837. I could probably dig further but I quit most things at the drop of a hat.

Example:

Henry: *"I can't just take vacation at the drop of a hat! My manager wants two weeks' notice."*

Or,

Heather: *"I'll tell Hank next week after we're gone."*

Heidi: *"Hank should know you're leaving him for Harry. Why wait?"*

Heather: *"Because Hank will hunt Harry at the drop of a hat when he finds out!"*

Brad says:

(*Drop Of a Hat*)

- They just weren't very tough in the 1800's now were they? If you 'knocked a chip off my shoulder,' I'd get miffed 'at the drop of a hat!'
- I think a hat falls slower to the ground than, say, a brick? "At the drop of a brick" sounds way better. Unless you're in a vacuum, then of course they fall at the same rate of speed. So, in space, "a drop of a hat" is just as fast as a "drop of a brick." I think this expression goes away once we conquer space and/or become tougher than the 1800's lads.
- Does the type of hat matter? I don't see anything menacing about a sombrero floating to the ground, so no urgency there. But drop a water soaked British Royal Guard hat and that means business!
- I wish there were more data on the origin because I just don't get this one. People must have used their headwear to signal immediate action, but then you'd either have to pick it up before you started your action or come back and get it. Should have been something like, "at the snap of my fingers" or simply, "Go."

The Early Bird Gets the Worm

Explanation:

This is a proverb meaning success comes to those who start early or first. If you want to be successful do it early, start soon, don't put it off any longer.

History:

From John Ray's *"A Collection of English Proverbs"* in the 1670's and was in the form:

"The early bird catcheth the worm."

(I wisheth we still spoketh that way.)

Example:

Coworker: *"You sure are here early, Nancy."*

Nancy: *"Big presentation today and I plan on nailing it. The early bird gets the worm, and I'm the early bird!"*

Or…

Son: *"I got cut from the team, Dad."*

Dad: *"I'm sorry, son. Maybe next year you can work harder, get up earlier, get to the gym before anyone else and be the early bird that gets the worm."*

Or…

Wife: *"I want that job sooooo bad!"*

Husband: *"Then you better apply soon, the early bird gets the worm."*

Brad says:

(The Early Bird Gets the Worm)

- Great for the bird, not so much for the worm.
- That's why worms live under ground, they're afraid of birds.
- You know that saying, "*The only thing we have to fear is fear itself*"? Franklin Delano Roosevelt said that, not a worm. Fear the bird!
- The late worm gets to wake up late tomorrow.
- What do late birds do for food?

Eating Crow

Explanation:

If you are "eating crow", figuratively speaking, you are publicly admitting you did or said something wrong. Assuming crow tastes bad and that it's probably tough and chewy at the same time and tastes nothing like chicken, eating crow would be a hard thing to do. Similar to how admitting when you're wrong is hard to swallow, crow is probably the same.

History:

Unknown by me. However, unreliable research says that an incident during the War of 1812 might have been the first time someone reportedly at crow. A British soldier found an American hunter and made him eat a crow he had just shot or he would end the young hunter's life. That American escaped, got his musket back and made the British soldier eat crow by shooting him in the face. Only one crow was harmed in this historical example.

Example:

> **Crazy Denver Broncos Fan:** *"I guess I was wrong saying the Broncos were going to win Super Bowl 48. Guess I'll be eating crow by getting that Seahawk tattoo on my chest and going shirtless to every Denver home game next year."*

Brad says:

(*Eating Crow*)
- It tastes like dirty, mean chicken.
- I think it would be hard for someone to admit they were wrong while physically eating a crow. Especially a live one. It would be hard for the listener because I think all I could focus on would be the bird fighting the guys' face in an effort

not to be eaten. Awesome! *"Say more wrong things next week, dude! I could watch this all night!"*

- I'm guessing crow tastes bad, otherwise what's so wrong with eating crow? And why do I have to do it when I'm wrong about something? I feel like the consequences for apologizing for something I did or said shouldn't be so harsh; for me or the crow. Who's ever going to want to admit being wrong? Now, if you had to "eat feces" then you'd make extra effort to not be wrong in the first place.

- *"You know what? I was wrong; this crow actually tastes delicious."*

- There's no wonder why kids don't want to ask questions in class. School lunches are bad enough, but to also have to eat a crow every time you get an answer wrong. I'm fairly certain those burgers in elementary were crowburgers anyway.

- We're horrible people. Seems to be a lot of anger against animals. We eat crow when we're wrong, we skin cats, and we let birds eat worms. But I guess that last one is ok, something's gotta eat those worms. And I guess we like to 'gift horses' and of course things are great, just like a bee's knees. If you're like me, you're hoping the rest of this book is more animal friendly.

An Empty Vessel Makes the Most Noise

Explanation:

Refers to people who talk a lot and express their opinion but are not necessarily intelligent or base those opinions on factual information. Sometimes, people with the least knowledge will talk the most. Someone may boast about their skills and/or abilities but can't perform to those expectations.

History:

Looks to be a proverb from English author William Baldwin but William Shakespeare used it in Henry V;

"I did never know so full a voice issue from so empty a heart: but the saying is true, the empty vessel makes the greatest sound."

Example:

You: *"I read this book about idioms, proverbs, and sayings and I just don't get it."*

Me: *"What do you mean?"*

You: *"The guy who wrote it claims to know a bunch of stuff but he really doesn't. But, you know what they say; an empty vessel makes the most noise, I guess."*

Me: <blink, blink> *"I don't know what that means. A vessel?"*

Brad says:

(*An Empty Vessel Makes the Most Noise*)

- Ummm, no it doesn't. It's empty, soooo...
- Maybe YOUR empty vessel makes a noise. But I'm pretty sure something empty is quiet.
- Well, my mother used to say this all the time about me. She said I talk a lot, I even say things that others have said were stupid but I know that when I am talking I sound wonderful and the things I say people like to hear so I'm not really sure what this one is all about. And I know most everything about anything, so this one was just a waste of my time. Makes me want to scream and just make all kinds of noise! SHEEESH!
- Unless you put a crying baby in a vessel with a bunch of hornets… But even then, I guess the "vessel" wouldn't be the thing making much noise. Babies and hornets should not be contained together.
- I guess I'm hoping this empty vessel makes the most noise by selling a ton of books!

Face the Music

Explanation:

Accepting the consequences of your actions. If you have to "face the music," you've probably done or said something wrong and now you have to atone for those actions by 'facing the music' or facing the consequences.

History:

No official origin to cite. An early 19th century American saying for accepting the punishment for something you have done. It could possibly be from early acting when actors were to face the orchestra in the front of the stage. Also, court marshaled solders might "face the music" when they were "drummed out of the military" – a literal drum squad would be playing during this practice.

Example:

Your Dad: "*I told you son; if you didn't get your grades up, I was going to take your car. Give me the keys, it's time to face the music.*"

You: "*As long as it isn't your music.*"

Your Dad: "*What?*"

You: "*Nothin' here ya go.*"

Brad says:

(*Face the Music*)

- Face the music because it's usually easier to hear and the lead singer is probably smokin' HOT!
- I wish my punishments as a young lad were simply "facing music." My spankings were so hard as a kid that I'd get spanked again for stretching out dad's belts.

- Unless that music is Yodelers yodeling, then it's better to just live with whatever you did wrong—even if it was killing Yodelers. We're all better off.
- I'd like to see gang members go with this sort of retort when confronting another thug, "*Yo, dawg, you're gonna face the music now.*" I think this type of comeback would help minimize killings and increase confusion.
- This one is a bit like eating crow, with less vomiting.
- It's possible to face the music while eating crow. Didn't Ozzy sing a song while eating a bat? Same-same.

Going To Hell in a Handbasket

Explanation:

This phrase refers to something that is deteriorating rather quickly. It could be an item that is aging and falling apart, or a dire situation that keeps getting worse. It could even be used to describe someone's appearance.

History:

This depends on your pickiness for detail. *"Head in a handbasket"* was printed in Samuel Sewall's Diary in 1714 but did not mention the *'going to hell'* part. The actual full phrase of *"going to hell in a handbasket"* is of U.S. origin in the middle of the 19th century.

Why the handbasket? Well, that's the thing at the bottom of the guillotine that catches the heads. Guillotines were used to decapitate criminals and the "perps" were probably going to hell.

Example:

> **Me Lying About My Legs:** *"Ever since I broke my legs, I can't exercise as effectively and now my whole body is going to hell in a handbasket."*

Or,

> **Me Not Wanting To Paint The House:** *"Just look at it! I haven't fixed the roof, cleaned the gutters or painted in years. The house is going to hell in a handbasket."*

Brad says:

(Going To Hell in a Handbasket)

- Going to hell? In a handbasket? Sounds like a pretty bougie way to travel considering you're going to hell. Wait, is this basket on fire!?
- *"My car keeps breaking down. It's going to hell in a hand basket."* That doesn't even make sense... Even if hell is real and handbaskets are favored there, what does it have to do with things deteriorating faster? Fail.
- You go to hell your way; I'll go to hell my way.
- Handbasket. I can't help thinking of this scene: Little Red Riding Hood skiping through the woods full of joy, a full handbasket swinging to and fro. As she travels the familiar path to her Grandma's house, her carefree spirit seems to nourish the dark forest with joy, young life, and vigor. Flowers flourish and bloom, grasses green, woodland creatures frolic. But wait, what's this? OH no! A wolf stops her in her tracks.

    "What's in the basket, little girl?" Snarls the Big Bad Wolf.

    Little Red sheepishly grins as she raises the basket face level and blows across the top of the basket lifting the doily and exposing the contents. The wolf pauses, his slobber subsides as his eyes gloss over at the site of his own wolf cub puppies staring back at him. Their little eyes empty, scared, and very dead. He glances back up at Little Red. She winks,

    "The rest of them were delicious." Little Red says as she wipes her lips.
- I think technology would have helped for storage and transport services in the mid-19th century. You know how an MRI takes many layered pictures of your innards? Well, the same concept would have been great with guillotine

technology. Slam! Raise blade. Move the perp forward a bit. Slam! Raise blade. Move the perp forward a bit, repeat. You could slice the heads in deli-thin slices making the storage and transport of several heads in a single handbasket. If you wanna move down the ladder in hell, you gotta think inside the handbasket.

➤ Shouldn't it be called a headbasket?

Good Things Come In Small Packages

Explanation:

This saying implies that small packages may contain more valuable things than larger packages. It's not always the largest package that will have the best item. Sometimes this proverb will be used in reference to short people who have done extraordinary things. Spud Webb, Wes Welker, Pele? All studs at 5'6", 5'9", 5'8" respectively. Just like a watermelon Jolly Rancher, these great things came in small packages.

Engagement/Wedding rings in small boxes may have more intrinsic meaning to someone than a gift in a bigger package like an automobile. Of course, we all know that's silly and we'd take the car. Just imagine a child on his birthday standing in front of two presents, one is the size of a deck of cards, the other one the size of an unmade bicycle. He can choose only one. The child is going to choose the bicycle box, or whatever is in it. 'Course it wasn't a bicycle- it was a freaking night stand for my bedroom. What the hell? Who gets furniture for their 6th birthday? This guy. The other gift? 50 US dollars. That one hurt.

History:

I couldn't find any history on this saying. I'm going to say that someone was bitter when they opened their small tin of Almond Roca and saw just a few small candies. When they popped that thing in their mouth they exclaimed, *"This thing kicks peanut brittle's ass! Delicious! Looks like good things do come in small packages."* -- Brad Myers 1974

Example:

> **Girl Who Likes Bears:** *"You know good things come in small packages, why'd you choose that over what clearly looked like a ring box?"*

Girl Who Hates Bears: "*I thought it was going to be a puppy, not this stupid stuffed bear riding a unicycle.*"

Girl Who Likes Bears: "*Can I have it? I'll name him Rider, and teach him about appreciation.*"

Brad says:

(*Good Things Come In Small Packages*)

➢ Except paychecks.
➢ Except penises.
➢ Except boobs.

Go Off Half Cocked

Explanation:

This phrase means to act or speak without preparation. To go into action without thinking fully. In an argument you might 'go off half-cocked' and say something in the heat of the argument because you are mad, excited and not prepared. You might say something you regret later because you 'went off half-cocked.'

History:

Old flintlock firearms used a cock to strike a spark to fire the gun. When the gun was set at half-cock, it was safe. When set at full-cock, it was ready to fire. If the gun ever fired from half-cock it was a mistake, a misfire or premature firing.

In the early 1700's going off half-cocked referred to firearms. By the late 1700's the term half-cocked referred to being drunk:

Fergus Hume's *Madame Midas: a story of Australian mining life*, 1888, explained the term:

> "*This last drink reduced Mr. Villiers to that mixed state which is known in colonial phrase as half-cocked.*"

It isn't until 1800's that the saying took the meaning it has today which is to speak or act impulsively.

"To-day in Ireland", 1825:
"*Master Dillon - never let an insult go off half-cock.*"

"The Register of Debates in Congress", 1833, recorded the opinions of Dutee Pearce of Rhode Island:
"*I regret that the gentleman from Maryland has gone off half-cocked.*"

Example:

Son: "*Dad, I am so mad at her, I just want to call her right now and tell her I never want to see her again!*"

Dad: "*Careful, son. You don't want to go off half-cocked and regret something you say or do. Take some time, think about it, you might find you will want to see her again. Don't ruin your relationships with harsh words you can't take back.*"

Or,

Wife speaking with her friend: "*I told him to sit down, think through all the issues and possibilities before firing him. But no, he went off half-cocked and fired the guy- Now there's a lawsuit because he didn't follow proper firing procedures!*"

Brad says:

(*Go Off Half Cocked*)

- Also known as "50% chub."
- The Seven Dwarfs.
- Men and women can agree that being half-cocked is the worst thing that can ever happen, to either of you.
- John Wayne Bobbitt.

Hair of the Dog

Explanation:

Hair of the dog is the act of drinking more alcohol in an attempt to cure your hangover from the irresponsible choices you made the night before. The belief is that if you apply more alcohol to your system, the system will respond by picking up where you left off. Science! I mean, "Stupid!" However, if you've ever been to 'dog town' you know it works because you start getting drunk again. But everybody at work knows you're drunk again and you're just prolonging the inevitable.

History:

"Hair of the dog that bit us" is from the medieval belief that when bitten by a rabid dog you should apply the hair from the same rabid dog to the wound to heal it. We now know that to be the understandings of very simple folk. Everyone knows that if you are bit by a rabid dog you just need to put a little butter on it and walk it off.

So, where did the phrase come from? Once again John Heywood and his ""*A dialogue conteinying the number in effect of all the proverbes in the Englishe tongue"* in 1546 comes to the rescue:

> "*I pray thee let me and my fellow have a hair of the dog that bit us last night. And bitten were we both to the brain aright. We saw each other drunk in the good ale glass.*"

Example:

Me: "*I drank way too much last night, I'm so hung-over!*"

You: "*What you need is a little hair of the dog, let me fix you a Bloody-Mary.*"

Me: *"I'm gonna throw up."*

Brad says:

(*Hair of the Dog*)

- ➤ I've tried licking the back of my dog to cure my hangover. Note: I was probably still drunk and it didn't work and dogs literally taste like shit. Well, dogs like mine do, the kind who roll on their backs in their own shit. Your mileage may vary. Don't lick your dog!
- ➤ I've also tried rum & cola to cure a rum & cola hangover. If getting drunk again at 9am is the cure to a hangover I'd rather just not stop drinking.
- ➤ Oddly enough, this practice does work for some people in that it prolongs the symptoms, but doesn't cure. So, if your body is mostly made up of alcohol, apply more, repeat. You'll be self-embalmed when they put you in your hole.
- ➤ I've had hangovers where I'm pretty sure getting rabies would be less painful.

I Am A Bit Under The Weather

Explanation:

This is just a softer way to say you aren't feeling well. It can apply to many variations of not feeling well: sick, menstruating, headache, don't want to go to work, etc.

History:

Nautical. Originally it just represented being seasick. The actual statement was 'under the weather bow' because the bow is where the worst weather is coming from. Seasick sailors would be sent below where they were under the deck and thus 'under the weather.'

Example:

Boss: *"Are you coming in to work today? We started at the usual time."*

You: *"I'm feeling a bit under the weather today. I think I'll be better tomorrow."*

Brad says:

(*I Am A Bit Under The Weather*)

- ➤ Isn't everyone? Unless you're in an airplane or spaceship, then you might be over the weather.
- ➤ I don't think going lower in the boat is going to help me. I need to throw up on land. I'd like land, please.
- ➤ When I "call in sick," I just tell them that I'm farting oddly and I don't know where it's headed. They're ok with me staying home.
- ➤ "Can't make it in today, boss…I'm under the weather." <<In Hawaii!!!>>

- Another great stripper name: "Can't make it in, boss. I've been Under The Weather all night."

I Am All Ears

Explanation:

Listening intently. If you're 'all ears' you're doing nothing else but listening to what's being said.

History:

No history. Well, some guy on the Internet stated it was "…at least 3 centuries old." Even I won't just blurt out obscure references that cover at least 300 possibilities- and I identify as "lazy." So, in a pinch, when someone asks you when this happened, just tell them, "300 or so years ago." And if you're in a pinch like that, where you're arguing with someone about how long ago a saying was made, you're probably used to getting beat up. Keep your hands up, protect your face!

Here, I'll make this easy by making my own history you can use for situations like that. The reader is encouraged to find the real history if interested, but here's mine…

It was a long, sunny day of the summer of 5,000 B.C. and everything was … Well, everything just basically 'was' at this time in history. This phrase originated in a corn field and first stated by Isaac Stalk when he was asked a simple, but direct question, *"Do you have a minute to hear me out?"* His response was what you would expect when one corn stalk speaks to another, *"I'm all ears."*

Yep, I just did that.

Example:

Your Girlfriend: *"I really need your attention right now. I'm going to tell you all about my day!"*

You, Lying: *"Go ahead, I'm all ears."*

Or,

Squad Leader: *"Now listen up everyone. This mission will be the most important one in your life. For the next 3 minutes I want you to be all ears."*

Brad says:

(*I Am All Ears*)

- *"Ow! Could you keep it down a bit? You're really loud."*
- I think I'd be happier being all penis.
- Nobody says, "I'm all ears" when they want to imply they are listening intently. They usually say, "*What*?"
- I dated a girl that was all ears. That was a disappointing 3 days.
- Guys are all ears until girls are all boobs. We're all pigs.
- What would you choose, all ears or all thumbs? I think you can do more with thumbs than you can with ears.

I Cried Because I Had No Shoes Until I Saw a Man Who Had No Feet

Explanation:

This Persian proverb helps you understand that your lot in life isn't as bad as it may seem, it could always be worse. Regardless of your situation in life, be thankful for what you have and can do. So work on fixing what you can, in this case; get some shoes.

History:

From the Persian poet Sa'di in his work *"Gulistan"* which translates to "The Rose Garden." Written in 1258, *"Gulistan"* is a collection of stories and poems and is considered a source of wisdom. This saying is paraphrasing story 19 from the *"Gulistan"*

> *I never lamented about the vicissitudes of time or complained of the turns of fortune except on the occasion when I was barefooted and unable to procure slippers. But when I entered the great mosque of Kufah with a sore heart and beheld a man without feet I offered thanks to the bounty of God, consoled myself for my want of shoes and recited:*
>
> > *'A roast fowl is to the sight of a satiated man*
> > *Less valuable than a blade of fresh grass on the table*
> > *And to him who has no means nor power*
> > *A burnt turnip is a roasted fowl.'*

Example:

You might say this to someone who is overly critical of their "miserable" situation:

Them: *"I can't believe they only have Chardonnay, I can only drink Pinot! What am I possibly going to do?!"*

You: *"You're an idiot. I cried once when I had no shoes, until I saw a woman with no feet. And she was drinking Chardonnay just fine."*

Brad says:

(*I Cried Because I Had No Shoes Until I Saw a Man Who Had No Feet*)

- Right, that's fine, he has no feet. But he also doesn't NEED shoes. I do.
- I cried because I had no shoes until I saw a man who had no feet…And <u>that</u> man cried because he had no feet until he saw a man who had no eyes. And that man cried—well, he couldn't cry because he had no eyes, but he would have cried if he could. So he just laughed and pointed erringly at the two guys who had no shoes or feet.
- How do you meet a man who has no feet? I think you have to be actively looking for someone with no feet. This isn't something you just come across, like someone with a similar hair style. Your life sucks so you go out and look for someone worse off so you can say, *"Sucks to be you."* You also have no soul (get it? Soul like sole… The bottom of a shoe!!!).
- But I STILL don't have any shoes, why doesn't anyone care about that?
- Share your shoes with others. That can be a metaphor for taking care of each other. No matter how bad you have it, it can always be worse. Unless you're dead, then it really can't be worse for you. Give generously to each other.

If You Can't Say Anything Nice, Don't Say Anything At All.

<<This space is intentionally left blank>>

It's Not Over Until the Fat Lady Sings

Explanation:

Nothing is finished until the final action is taken. You shouldn't assume that something is over until a clearly defined outcome has occurred. The team that is behind in the score still has a chance to win until the final whistle. A race car hasn't lost until someone crosses the finish line. The opera isn't over until the final song and/or scene.

History:

<suspendHate>

This is not the most sensitive topic so please suspend your hate. Many operas will conclude with a solo. Often, this solo figure is rotund or hefty (sometimes large by costume, sometimes large by genetics, sometimes large by burgers and fries). When this person's solo was finished, the opera was over. Many of these operas employed a woman for this solo role and in fact, some men dressed as women to perform this role. <<< Did opera just get more interesting? >>>.

Some operas lasted 12 or more hours! The only thing I have ever done for 12 or more hours is breathe. So the answer to a question like,

"When is this thing going to be over?" would be,

"When the fat lady sings."

Since it wasn't a particular 'fat lady' nor a particular opera, we don't know the date for this expression. However, it was American sports casters in the latter half of the 20th century who popularized it. During exciting comebacks in sporting events, sports casters would blurt out something to the effect,

"Hold on folks! That's 21 points in the last 3 minutes, they are making a march! It ain't over until the fat lady sings!"

Example:

Soccer Coach: *"Ok ladies, we're getting killed out there but the score is only 11-0. Let's get out there in the second half and get those scores back- it's not over until the fat lady sings... Sorry, Alice."*

Brad says:

(*It's Not Over Until the Fat Lady Sings*)

- ➢ Sometimes it is over before the fat lady sings, like when you left the opera after the very first song because operas are boring.
- ➢ Remember the Seattle band, "*Heart*?" Ann and Nancy Wilson rocked the stage! They still do! Man, they were great in concert. Yep. Rock and Roll in the mid 70's was strong. And then they seemed to stop playing for a while and then resurfaced in the late 80's and 90's. They were louder and bigger than before and, well, you know what age does to all of us. You couldn't tell when their more recent concerts were over because Ann was always singing.
- ➢ It's not over when the fat lady sings because I end up spending the next 20 minutes bitching about how boring the opera was.
- ➢ I've been in several games where most of us on the team felt it was over because we were losing so badly. You know what I do in cases like that? I start singing. Everyone gets to go home.

</suspendHate>

A Leopard Cannot Change Its Spots

Explanation:

This biblical phrase is used to describe someone who cannot change who they are. Usually used to refer to someone's personality or nature or even their pattern of behavior.

History:

This is from King James Bible, Jeremiah 13:23,

> *"Can an Ethiopian change his skin or a leopard its spots? Neither can you do good who are accustomed to doing evil."*

Example:

Cindy: *"I think it'll be ok. Chester went to a doctor and I really think he'll stop hitting me now."*

Martha: *"Oh Cindy, a leopard cannot change its spots, Chester will hurt you again. You must leave!"*

Or,

Chester: *"Cindy will take me back."*

Jordan: *"What makes you say that, you beat the shit out of her!"*

Chester: *"Because she's a sweetheart and a leopard cannot changes its spots."*

Brad says:

(A Leopard Cannot Change Its Spots)

- I wonder why they picked on leopards in the Bible writing days? They aren't necessarily evil…Well, I guess all cats are but there must have been an influx of leopard killings back then. Zebras have stripes so that would've flowed nicely, too. "A zebra cannot change its stripes." Dalmatians have spots but I wonder if they were around before that movie came out—weren't there like 100 of them things? Spots are funny.

- I Googled some images of spots and it turns out they got this one right! Leopards are bad-ass! They aren't really mean, they are just constantly looking for meat. So, I can see why they misinterpreted their hunger for evil.

- I don't get this one. I wonder if the leopard ever wanted to change its spots? Does the leopard question its place in the food chain based on its outward appearance? Does the leopard have crushing self-doubt? I just don't know. It's still a cat so it most likely doesn't give a shit but cats do care about their appearance. If it could change its spots it'd still be an asshole- only because it's still a cat.

- So in Biblical times, people thought cats were mean and evil. Still true today. I'd insert an image of a cat with tears but there aren't any. They just don't care.

Let the Cat Out Of the Bag

Explanation:

If you've let the cat out of the bag, you've probably told a secret you were supposed to keep to yourself. Sharing information that was not to be shared is "letting the cat out of the bag."

History:

Dates back to medieval marketplaces where farmers would sell piglets in a sack.

"Sixpence for a bag-of-pigs. Get your bag-of-pigs, now!"

The farmers would open their sacks to show customers the piglets. Sometimes, unscrupulous farmers (entrepreneurs) who had a bad 'pig-year', would try to pass off baby kittens as piglets.

Customer: *"That one sounds like a kitten."*

Farmer: *"I think that was just a cough. He has a cold."*

Customer: *"No, that was definitely a meow."*

Farmer: *"Ohhh, yeah, that pig ate a kitten this morning. I won't charge you extra."*

The customers that called the bad farmers out on their devious behavior were said to be letting the cat out of the bag because they would literally let the cat out of the bag. Not in the case above where the pig had eaten the kitten. That kitten is dead. If it makes you feel any better, the pig is dead and eaten by now, too. And, in case you were wondering; pig tastes better than kitten.

Example:

> **Mary Lou**: *"The surprise party would have been awesome had Kevin not let the cat out of the bag yesterday when he asked me if I was going to be there!"*

Brad says:

> (*Let the Cat Out Of the Bag*)

- However, there is another saying that's easier to follow because you don't have to do anything:
    - *"The only good cat IS a cat in a bag."*
- Every cat needs a good, closeable, bag.
- Certainly a practice we could all do a little more of-- if you see a cat in a bag, let it out!
- It really depends on the size of the bag and the size of the cat in the bag. You might want to just keep the bag closed and walk away.
    - Cougar? Keep it closed!
    - Lion? Keep it closed!
    - Hairless cat? Keep it closed!
    - Cat? Meh, do what you will.
    - Kitten? Let the cat out of the bag!!!

Note: No pigs, lions, cougars, or house cats (full-grown) were harmed in this writing. The kitten is still eaten, unfortunately, and so is that one pig, but not because of this writing.

Like A Bull in a China Shop

Explanation:

This idiom refers to being awkward in a delicate situation. This could mean something physical like a clumsy child stampeding down a crystal sculpture aisle in the store. Or it could be something verbal if someone says something awkward in a serene setting. Asking if a woman is pregnant when she isn't is like being as clumsy as a bull in a china shop.

History:

Early nineteenth century, maybe 1812ish? There might be an example in 1841, I don't really know, seems like the Internet doesn't know either. You figure it out. We do know it was old enough to have store fronts which sold china and a time when free range bulls roamed the streets.

Example:

> **Me On A Date:** "... *And then I reached across the table to get the salt and knocked over a beer, some wine, and rolled a roll into the butter bowl. Bull in a china shop they call me. Bull in a china shop. It happens all the time... Hey, pass the salt.*"
>
> **Her Looking For An Exit Strategy:** "*I have to go.*"
>
> **Me On A Date:** "*Split the check?*"

Brad says:

> (*Like A Bull in a China Shop*)

> ➢ Seems like a mean attack on bulls here. They seem pretty agile to me, and if you're letting one in your china shop then

I... Wait, who owns a china shop AND a bull? Sounds like poor business planning but yet strangely awesome!

➤ <scene: We're at a funeral together.>

> **Me**: "*I never know the right things to say at these funerals. Right now, I really feel like a bull in a china shop.*"
>
> **You**: "*What? Why would you feel like a bull in a china shop?*"
>
> **Me**: "*Because, look across the street, there's a bull in that china shop, and he's really scared and sad. That's how I feel.*"
>
> **You**: "*You should really be saying things about your mother right now, everyone is staring.*"

➤ If I were a bull browsing in a china shop and people were saying, "*Ewwww a bull in a china shop and he's clumsy!*" and pointed at me and ran away, I'd break some damn china too!

A Little Bird Told Me

Explanation:

Usually used in response to when you've shared something you weren't supposed to and you want to keep the source anonymous. Why a little bird? Because of all the creatures on the planet, birds are the worst gossipers.

History:

The actual text isn't in any version of the Bible, but some point to Ecclesiastes 10-20 (King James Version):

> "*Curse not the king, no not in thy thought; and curse not the rich in thy bedchamber: for a bird of the air shall carry the voice, and that which hath wings shall tell the matter.*"

So, you're saying I should curse the bird? I thought you weren't supposed to shoot the messenger? I never understood Biblease.

Of course, Shakespeare and other authors make reference to birds sending messages, including Frederick Marryat in his *Peter Simple*, 1833: "*A little bird has whispered a secret to me.*" But if you're like me, you've stopped reading because you're still giggling about Fred's title of "*Peter Simple.*"

All birds are liars, everyone knows that. So, if you're going to share a secret, just tell people a bird told you. It makes complete sense and everyone understands. You know how I know? ... That's right! A little bird told me.

Example:

Mary: "*Did you hear that Alice is pregnant?*"

Jane: "*How do you know that?*"

Mary: "*I can't tell you, let's just say a little bird told me.*"

Jane: "*Was the bird's name, Alice? It was, wasn't it?*"

Brad says:

(*A Little Bird Told Me*)

- If you can hear birds talking then you should consider travelling around with a Carnival. Carnies get lots of tail, and if you're hearing birds talking and share that with Carnival friends, you'll get top-notch Carny tail! Do they still have traveling carnivals? They should. I'm bringing Carnivals back. That and Zot's candy- and Pop Rocks!
- If birds are telling you things, write them down, you definitely want to know what they're saying for your court hearing when smarter people beat you up for being crazy.
- Really? A bird told you she was pregnant? Well, is that bird going to get a job and support that bastard child?
- If the bird told you someone was pregnant then the bird probably did it. You should sleep with fewer birds and take more or less medication.
- If birds are telling secrets, there is only one secret I really want to know about… And that is: "*How can I learn to fly?*"

A Little Knowledge/Learning Is a Dangerous Thing

Explanation:

Having a little knowledge about something can make people think they know more about a subject than they really do.

Sometimes people learn a little about a topic and then act as the expert on that topic. The danger is in not fully understanding your topic and then trying to teach others when you aren't fully equipped... Present 'author' entirely included.

History:

Credited to Alexander Pope (1688 – 1744) *An Essay on Criticism*, 1709. But that was a long time ago and something you're never going to read. But he's credited with "*To err is human; to fogive, divine*" and "*For fools rush in where angels fear to tread.*" So here's a copy/paste from "*An Essay on Criticism.*"

> "*A little learning is a dang'rous thing;*
> *Drink deep, or taste not the Pierian spring:*
> *There shallow draughts intoxicate the brain,*
> *And drinking largely sobers us again.*"

I've had to read that a few times to understand it. It's actually pretty brilliant and I resonate with the last line because I do believe it is 'the hair of the dog' that fixes a hangover.

Examples:

Me: "*Hey did you read my book on idioms and sayings?*"

You: "*No, is it any good?*"

Me: "*Not really, but I learned a lot and now I'm the expert on all things said.*"

You: *"My friend read your book, and it appears that a little knowledge IS a dangerous thing because he thinks you're an idiot and pretending to know stuff. He says you're making people dumber."*

Me: *"Consistency has always been a strength of mine."*

Brad says:

(*A Little Knowledge/Learning Is a Dangerous Thing*)

- I don't think anyone said this to Robert Oppenheimer.
- This might have happened:

    Brother: *"Hey, I know that if I drop this rock from up here, it will fall on your head."*

    Younger Brother: *"Don't!"*

    <Drops rock>

    Younger Brother: *"OUCH!"*

    Brother: *"Geez! Sorry, I had no idea a little knowledge would be a dangerous thing."*

- …And that's the extent of my knowledge/learning on this topic. I just want to make sure everyone gets out alive.

A Man (Or Woman) After My Own Heart

Explanation:

A potential lover who agrees with your innermost desires might be someone who is 'after your own heart.' It describes someone who wants to be with you and win your heart in love. Someone who likes the same things you do, or wants and strives for the same outcomes could be considered someone after your own heart.

But then other times it's about harvesting organs and selling hearts on the black market. Don't sell hearts or harvest organs unless you're qualified which I guess is just someone with knives, motivation, and interested buyers. This got dark.

History:

From the Bible; Samuel 13:14:

"But now your kingdom will not endure; the Lord has sought out a man after his own heart and appointed him ruler of his people, because you have not kept the Lord's command."

Less about love back whenever that was, but the modern use is about love and finding that special someone who is after your heart. Let it happen. If you're lucky enough in this world to have someone love on you that much; take it, enjoy it, you probably deserve it.

Example:

Woman: *"He brought me flowers and candy the other day...And tonight, he's cooking me dinner."*

Bad Friend of Woman: *"You sure he's not just cheating on you?"*

Woman: "Nahhh *he's just a man after my own heart."*

Bad Friend of Woman: *"Flowers, candy, AND cooking dinner? Oh, he's definitely cheating on you."*

Woman: *"You're a bad friend, you need to leave."*

Brad says:

(*A Man (or woman) After My Own Heart*)

- Also describes a heart surgeon or cannibal.
- If a man or woman is "after your heart", it might be a euphemism for "after your money."
- I've been a man after a woman's heart but everyone knew I was really just after her sexy bits and pieces.
- Some women think the best way to a man's heart is through his stomach. Those women are alone. Cooking for him is fine, but you'll know when he's after your heart when he's treating you with respect, being kind and courteous, and pays all attention to you. … Yeah, I thought I was going in a different direction as well, but I stand by my statement.
- This one time, in college, I was working on a 'family tree' project with a woman I thought might be after my own heart because she told me I smelled nice. So, at break, I bought her a bouquet of flowers and told her, *"I hope they smell as good as I do."* and then I asked her out on a date. She smiled shyly and said, *"No, I said you spelled nice. "Spelled" not "smelled" – Sheesh, stop petting my hair!"* #restrainingorder

Man Does Not Live On Bread Alone

Explanation:

"People do not live on bread alone" is more acceptable. This biblical statement means that someone cannot live only on food, that other needs must be met to be happy and healthy. In particular, this biblical statement is in regards to faith and a relationship with your God that will help complete one's health.

Bread/Food is a primary sustenance but is not the only thing humans need to live. The use of the word 'live' is subjective as humans can live on only food and water for a remarkably long time. The word 'live' in this phrase is really used to describe an entire 'life' … In that a person cannot live a full and happy life on food alone. They need relationships with people and deities, with exercise and good mental health.

History:

Deuteronomy 8:3 New International Version (NIV):

> *"He humbled you, causing you to hunger and then feeding you with manna, which neither you nor your ancestors had known, to teach you that man does not live on bread alone but on every word that comes from the mouth of the Lord."*

Mathew 4:4 (NIV):

> *"Jesus answered, It is written: Man shall not live on bread alone, but on every word that comes from the mouth of God."*

And not to be outdone, Luke had something to add,

Luke 4:4 (NIV):

"Jesus answered, "It is written: Man shall not live on bread alone."

Example:

Brother, 9 years old: *"Are you going to drink the blood of Christ? You know it's wine, right?"*

Sister, 12 years old: *"Uh, yeah, man or woman does not live on bread alone."*

Or,

Daughter: *"I'm not going to church today. I have other things to do!"*

Mother: *"Man does not live on bread alone, you're going to church."*

Brad says:

(*Man Does Not Live On Bread Alone*)

- Man can live on bread alone; but it's a very dry and boring life.
- Man tried to live on bread alone and quickly realized that was a stupid idea. That's when Spam was invented, and all was right with the world.
- Words are great. And the word of God probably the most important for many. But I'd prefer a sandwich because I can't live on words alone.
- Every person needs more than bread and words to be healthy. Water is a good one…Oh, and Oxygen should be readily available. And my personal opinion: friends. I could die unhealthy but happy in the arms of a friend.

➤ Man can't live on bread alone. We need chicks… For the eggs when young and the meat when mature.

A Man's Got To Do What a Man's Got To Do

Explanation:

This phrase tells you to follow your conscience, whatever the consequences. This one is pretty sexist. Just think of it as reading like this: "A person's got to do what a person's got to do." Why didn't I make the title like that? Because a man's got to do what a man's got to do! Sheesh.

History:

Arguments abound over this one! Heaped in movie tradition and studly renditions, this saying was repeated by some of the best there ever was, or will be.

Some might say John Wayne said it best:

"*Well, there's some things a man just can't run away from.*"

And,

"*A man ought'a do what he thinks is best.*"

But those are actual quotes from John Wayne movies, "*Stagecoach*" and "*Hondo*", respectively. So they might be close but not an actual match.

John Steinbeck wrote a book in 1939 called "*The Grapes of Wrath*", and in that book there's a line that reads like this:

"*I hate catching spiders. Still, a man's got to do what a man's got to do.*"

That is SO not as tough as John Wayne saying it. Mostly because I'm reading it in my head and it's my cowardly voice—much like Alvin the Chipmunk using a speech jammer.

Is Charlton Heston more badass than John Wayne? Ask any planet with apes on them and they'll say a resounding, "oooh-ooh-hoo-oooh-hohooh-oooh" which is clearly ape for, "Probably." And, while Ben-Hur should have said it, he didn't. Still, Charlton Heston as Captain Colt Saunders is pretty badass with his line from the 1956 movie *"Three Violent People"*:

> …
> *"I need the drink, not the poetry."*
> *<No toast>*
> *"The insult is unnecessary, amigo."*
> *"A man must do what he must do."*
> …

Oh man! This is awesome – John freakin' Wayne and Charlton Heston battling it out for idiom etymology supremacy while a famous author, John Steinbeck is ignored? It doesn't get any better than… Oh, wait… NO sir, it <u>did</u> just get better, and case closed...

> *"Ha, 'a man's gotta do what a man's gotta do'. I should've won three space Oscar awards."*
>
> -- 1962, THE George Jetson

George Jetson: Winner.

Example:

> **Mom's friend:** *"So tell me again why your husband decided NOT to rent a log splitter. Why did he do it all by hand?"*
>
> **Mom:** *"You know what Carl's like - a man's gotta do what a man's gotta do. And apparently he had to do it the hard way."*

Brad says:

(A Man's Got To Do What a Man's Got To Do)

- This is man-code used to cover up for something stupid we did. For example, a man gets home from a weekend in Vegas where he was less than faithful:
    - **Lovely wife**: *"So, how was your weekend? I heard there were girls involved?"*
    - **Douche**: *"Honey, a man's gotta do what a man's gotta do."*
    - **Leaving wife**: *"Is that right? Well I had to do what I had to do, and it was your best friend, Charlie."*
- Sometimes what a man has to do is far easier than what a woman has to do. Men have it easy. For example, the systematic bleeding from your genitals on a monthly schedule is not something a man could endure.
- Being faithful, respectful, loving, caring, and nurturing to his wife, children, family, and friends is what a man has to do – Everything else is less than man…And nowhere near John Wayne or Charlton Heston. George Jetson? Well, he's from another world entirely.

A Man of Few Words

Explanation:

Someone who doesn't speak much.

History:

From William Shakespeare's *"King Henry V"* 1599:

"He hath heard that men of few words are the best men."

Example:

" ... "

Brad says:

(*A Man of Few Words*)

➢ Like this.

A Man Who Is His Own Lawyer Has a Fool for a Client

Explanation:

This proverb implies that if you represent yourself in court instead of hiring a real lawyer, you are a fool. A lawyer understands the courtroom procedures, protocol, and intricacies of the judicial system. You don't. Get a lawyer.

History:

Proverb – Early 19th century, the exact origin is nearly impossible since a lawyer probably said it, and you can't trust them, right? However, we could credit Henry Kett, in his 1814 book, *"The flowers of wit, or a choice collection of bon mots."*

"...*observed the eminent lawyer, I hesitate not to pronounce, that every man who is his own lawyer, has a fool for a client.*"

But again, it's been pointed out (by a lawyer, no doubt) that a very similar phrase was written five years earlier in the Philadelphia *Port Folio:*

"He who is always his own counselor will often have a fool for a client."

Author unknown, so, there is a discrepancy as to when it was originally published and by whom! Perhaps a couple of lawyers could get together at a bar and sort this out over snifters of arsenic. I'm not bitter.

Example:

Me: *"I'm going to represent myself in this murder case."*

You: *"You know a man who is his own lawyer has a fool for a client, right? Why would you do that? You don't know anything about the law."*

Me: *"Right, but I murdered my lawyer, soooo, sort of on my own here."*

You: <Blink, blink>

Brad says:

(*A Man Who Is His Own Lawyer Has a Fool for a Client*)

- If a lawyer represents himself he's also a fool.
- If a person represented himself as the authority on something (like, maybe idioms and phrases for example) wouldn't that person also be a fool? He is.
- I'd rather represent myself and be a fool than give credit to some lawyer. Hell, I'd rather spend my time in prison than have some well-educated, persistent person represent me and keep me home and safe with my family. Who's the fool? WHO'S THE FOOL, NOW!?!

Needle in a Haystack

Explanation:

Something that is remarkably difficult to find. A way to describe a nearly impossible situation. A haystack is a large pile of dried grass (hay). Finding a tiny needle in that pile would be difficult and mostly luck if you could find it.

History:

The oldest credited source is from a Chinese proverb over 2,000 years ago:

"*…to dive into the sea, to feel for a needle.*"

Example:

Guy With Money To Burn: "*Winning the lottery is like trying to find a needle in a haystack- your odds are about the same.*"

Or,

Maze Quitter: "*We're never going to get out of this maze, finding the exit is going to be like finding a needle in a haystack.*"

Or,

You Reading This Book: "*Trying to find the humor in this book is like trying to find a needle in a haystack.*"

Brad says:

(*Needle in a Haystack*)

- Seems like a silly place to keep your needles.
- Relatively speaking, it all depends on the size of your needle. Know what I'm sayin'?
- There's always a chance you'll find your needle on your first look. I think finding a specific needle in a needlestack would be more difficult, and painful. Ouch!
- What's a needle? Honestly, does anyone sew anymore?
- What's a haystack? I've seen rectangular bundles and big round danish-pastry-looking hay in fields before, but I think the days of just stacking your hay in a pile are over. We've come so far.
- Much like Lawn Darts, the neighborhood game of Finding the Needle in the Haystack had to be retired due to serious (and yet comical) injuries to children.

On The Wagon

Explanation:

If you are "on the wagon" you are abstaining from drinking alcohol.

History:

This is another phrase or saying that has a colorful, if not fictional, history. Some may find that being on the wagon was used to describe prisoners on their way to jail. It was said they were allowed one last drink so the wagon would stop at a saloon to let the prisoners wet their whistle one last time.

Another story has the Salvation Army picking up people who were drunk to help them on their way to sobriety. Although that story is also untrue, the reference to a wagon is real.

The real origin came at the turn of the 20th century and started as "on the water cart." Over time, it became "on the water wagon" and eventually shortened to just "on the wagon." A water cart (water wagon) was a horse drawn wagon with a large tank of water that was sprayed on the roads to keep dust down during traffic. During the temperance movement, men who took the pledge to quit drinking would say they would rather drink from the water cart than drink alcohol. So, they were "on the wagon" when they quit drinking alcohol.

The temperance movement was a big deal in the 19th and early 20th century. In Oberlin, Ohio in 1893, the "Anti-Saloon League" was founded and became a national organization just two years later in 1895. It was not the first temperance organization but probably the most powerful prohibition group in the United States. It was responsible for the passage of the 18th Amendment to the Constitution resulting in nationwide prohibition in 1920.

Prohibition is credited with the rise of organized crime and The Dukes of Hazard. Crime, Speakeasies, bootlegging all drove the desire for a more controlled, and taxable way to handle societal problems. Government took the booze and the people revolted in the form of huge crime organizations and running booze illegally.

Example:

> **Pete:** *"Looks like Chester got drunk and attacked another girl."*
>
> **Donald:** *"Oh no! I thought he was on the wagon? Is the girl ok?"*
>
> **Pete:** *"He was on the wagon but started drinking again. And yeah, his mom is ok."*

Brad says:

> (*On The Wagon*)

- ➤ "On the wagon" is pretty dated. You won't hear many people using it. But if you do hear someone say they are on the wagon, be sensitive to their cause and get the hell out! That person on the wagon is boring and probably headed to a snooze-fest of a party. You go get your drink and snack on somewhere else!
- ➤ I never knew the right term to represent my drinking. I didn't know if I was "on the wagon" or "off the wagon." Perhaps if I drank less, I'd be able to tell if I was on or off a wagon.
- ➤ Today, I think people say they are sober or that they are drying out. Some may refer to it as abstaining or sworn off liquor. I really haven't heard anyone say those terms because I don't associate with quitters and I don't like all the negativity.
- ➤ If you're drunk and say, "on the wagon" repeatedly, it starts to sound really funny. Actually, I just tried it and no it doesn't. It's not funny at all- and I've been drinking so I should know.

- When I picture people on the wagon I assume they are drunk and happy because everyone loves drunk wagon rides. But it's really the sober healthy people on the wagon because the drunk people fall off the wagon.

Peeping Tom

Explanation:

This saying is used to describe someone who spies on others; historically a male watching others undress or engage in sexual activity. Peeping Tom's of the mid to late 20th century were mostly dudes peeking in on neighbor's wives. An exercise which was frowned upon and you'd get a stern talking to if caught! These days if you are caught, the video of you being creepy lives on the Internet forever. Don't be creepy. Don't be Tom.

History:

This one is a bit sketchy: Lady Godiva disrobed and rode naked on her horse through Coventry in opposition to taxes imposed by her husband in 1040'ish. Townspeople were told to shutter their windows and stay indoors. Guess who bore a hole in his shutters to view the fair maiden's elegant form? Some guy named Tom.

The documented story written more than a century after that event (*Flores Historiarum* by Roger of Wendover) didn't mention anyone spying on Lady Godiva and it is unclear why the story included that. However, there is mention of Tom the Tailor in Coventry city accounts in 1773- maybe his family name is taking the blame for all Tom's?

Example:

…

…

…

<You couldn't tell but I was watching you look for some content here. Uuuhhhuhh, I like what you're wearing.>

Brad says:

(*Peeping Tom*)

- And "Tom's" everywhere for eternity will never hear the end of this. Too bad it wasn't a cool name like, "Jake the Snake" or "Frank the Tank". No, we are forever stuck with:
    - "Tom the Tool"
    - "Too Bad Tom"
    - "Tommy Mommy"
    - "Tom's Ta-Ta's"
    - "Camel Toe Tom"
- I think Victoria's Secret models should represent opposition to taxes in this manner today. I'd stand street side slow clapping their arrival. Then faster clapping, some more slow clapping, clapping, left hand only clapping, both hands alternate clapping…CLAP!
- Don't kid yourself; he wasn't the only dude "peeping." Next door to Tom was "Leering Lenny", across from him was, "Staring Stan" and his brother "Ogling Oscar". Just down the road on a rooftop sat "Peering Pete" while his teenage son stayed indoors and earned his title of "Wacky Wayne". So we should cut Tom's a break.
- Dudes need to stop being creeps and stop the peeps. Get your jollies from the Internet like the rest of us.

The Pen Is Mightier Than the Sword

Explanation:

The written word can be more powerful than a steel sword. Writing can be more effective than violence. The power to move people through the written word or speech is historically documented (Declaration of Independence, Emancipation Proclamation, Magna Carta, Constitution, Bill of Rights, etc.).

If someone tells you that the pen is mightier than the sword, they are suggesting an approach other than violence. Use your words. Of course, if your hands were cut off by someone's sword, a pen isn't going to help but a jumbo pack of bandages and a friend sure would come in 'handy.' Get it?

History:

People have made this reference throughout history as defiance against harsh, stone-hand rulers and governments. Earliest coined phrase comes from Edward Bulwer-Lytton in a play, *Richelieu; Or the Conspiracy in 1839*:

> *"True, This!*
> *Beneath the rule of men entirely great*
> *The pen is mightier than the sword. Behold*
> *The arch-enchanters wand! - itself a nothing!*
> *But taking sorcery from the master-hand*
> *To paralyze the Caesars, and to strike*
> *The loud earth breathless! Take away the sword;*
> *States can be saved without it!"*
>
> Source:
> https://archive.org/stream/richelieuorconsp00lytt#page/52/mode/2up/search/sword

And then there's our famous Shakespeare who wrote it in his 'special' way (read: barely perceptible) in *Hamlet* in 1582:

"... many wearing rapiers are afraid of goose-quills and dare scarce come thither."

And a few other people at different times in history wrote or said the same thing. But you don't really care unless you know the name. So, you'll recognize Thomas Jefferson and acknowledge that he sent a letter to Thomas Paine (the original T-Paine) in 1796 which included this nugget:

"Go on doing with your pen what in other times was done with the sword."

So, TJ just wanted T Paine to stab and slash people with his pen! Now that's fun history. Go stream today's T-Pain's *"Buy you a drank"* you'll be glad you did.

Example:

Penny: *"I say we go down there and toilet paper the whole house."*

Sammy: *"I have a better idea; let's write them a nasty letter and mail it to them!"*

Penny: *"You're not going to give me that, "the pen is mightier than the sword" thing again, are you? Because making them clean up TP on their house is way more satisfying."*

Or,

Shawn: *"I just wanna break all the windows in her car!"*

Steve: *"No, let's fill out a police report and hit her where it counts. Remember, the pen is mightier than the sword."*

Brad says:

(*The Pen Is Mightier Than The Sword*)

- Ummm, no it's not.
- This is just a passive aggressive way for weak people to get even.
- That must be one big, strong pen!
- Haven't you heard that sticks and stones may break my bones but words will never hurt me? Sticks and stones will break your bones! Fear the sword.
- But if I lop off your fingers with my sword, your pen is useless.
- Ok, then we duel! Have at thee with your mighty pen.
- If my pen is mightier than your sword…Wanna trade?
- Sometimes a pen really is mightier than a sword. Like when the sword is that little plastic cocktail pirate sword and is fighting one of those giant fountain pens with the stabby point. I think feathered quill trumps all pens in a fair fight.
- It's like the chicken or the egg conundrum. I needed a pen to write the phrase, "The pen is mightier than the sword." But I needed a sword to steal the pen from an unarmed peasant. However, would that peasant be considered unarmed since he had the pen and no sword? An unarmed person has no use for a pen… or gloves, or sleeves. OH! That's why those down vests were invented; for people with no arms. Saves on material and looks better. Well done clothing technology.
- The sword is mightier for killing. The pen is mightier for coloring. The world needs more pens.

A Penny for Your Thoughts?

Explanation:

"A penny for your thoughts?" is a soft approach to asking someone what they are thinking or how they are feeling.

Typically, currency isn't exchanged for the thoughts, but sometimes holding out a penny for their thoughts is a good gesture. Besides, if you give them any advice in the transaction, ask for the penny back. Pennies were worth more back in the mid 1500's and sadly enough; so were people's thoughts.

History:

Once again, from the book written by John Heywood:

"A dialogue conteinying the nomber in effect of all the prouerbes in the Englishe tongue"

The title wasn't capitalized and seems to be spelled funny, but that's the way John Heywood rolled in 1546. The title was eventually shortened to *"The Proverbs of John Heywood"* by a less creative and lazier generation of humans.

John Heywood actually just wrote down all the things he heard in his travels, so he never claimed to have said *"A penny for your thoughts?"* However, since he was first to print it and there is no other information prior to his work, he gets the blame for this one.

If it helps you find a little respect for the lesser-known John Heywood, his early years as a playwright helped set the stage for playwrights like William Shakespeare.

Example:

Your daughter sits on her day bed looking longingly out the bay window. She seems sad. You want to know what she's thinking. Instead of yelling at her, "Whazzupppp!?" You might lead with this:

Dad: *"Everything ok, darling?"*

Daughter: *"I guess."*

Dad: *"Maybe I can help. Penny for your thoughts?"*

Daughter: *"What?"*

Dad: *"It's an expression."*

Daughter: *"I think you're a goof and you embarrass me."*

Dad: *"Yeah, sorry. Us dads say some silly things. Soooo, do you want that penny? Care to tell me what you're thinking?"*

Daughter: *"I just did."*

Brad says:

(*A Penny for Your Thoughts?*)

- If anyone says this to you, your first response should be, *"Yeah, ok, sure, thanks."* Stick out your hand and don't say anything until you feel that warm copper resting in your palm. They can go make change if need be! Keep a straight face and never waver.
- Smarter people will hold out for a whole dollar or more before saying anything.
- Someone may be in deep thought, and a friendly gesture like this may get you punched in the face.
- Offering currency to someone for information they may be reluctant to share is also known as extortion or a bribe.
- I give my thoughts based on the amount given. If it's a penny and I'm asked what I'm thinking, I'll say something like, *"I'm thinking about a friend."* If it's a dollar or more, I might get more specific, like, *"I'm thinking about your girlfriend."*

➢ I don't think people say dated things like this anymore. It just sounds old and at the very least makes you sound old. Next time you wonder what someone is thinking and you've got a few spare pennies, just mind your own damn business and keep your goofy sayings to yourself. They might be thinking they want to kill you.

A Penny Saved Is A Penny Earned

Explanation:

This English proverb means saving your money is just as good as earning more money. Frugality is the root here, and saving your money is almost like getting it twice. Meaning, you could spend the whole $50 or save $10 and only spend $40. Later, that $10 saved is sort of like an extra $10 earned. Hey, I'm just explaining what these things mean, it's not my math, it's probably common core related. Save your money. For example, maybe you don't buy this book and get yourself a latte and bagel instead.

History:

This proverb is credited to English poet, George Herbert in his *"Outlandish Proverbs"* in the early 17th century. Who was George Herbert? He was one of those 17th century poets you read about in high school and didn't care then and don't care now.

However, if you were born in England, this cat was da bomb! Not only was he a top notch poet, he excelled in languages and music at Trinity College Cambridge and eventually would hold prestigious teaching positions. He spent two years in Parliament until politics bored him. He then became a devoted Christian and cared for the English people much more than they cared for their own teeth. See? I paid attention in school for some stuff, just not the right stuff.

Some research will tell you that Benjamin Franklin said it-- but that's because everyone thought Ben Franklin was poor; mostly in part due to his chain of crappy, yet fun to shop at, convenience/craft stores. It's unclear why Ben Franklin is wrongly credited with this proverb and there is no hard evidence to suggest he did. So, George Herbert wrote it, and Ben Franklin just macramé'd the words and glued them to a piñata and sold it for $14.99.

Ben Franklin: Winner!

Example:

> **Your Son**: *"Dad, I really want that string-less yo-yo and they're only asking a penny for it!"*
>
> **You:** *"Son, if you save that penny today, you might save enough pennies to buy a yo-yo with a string. A penny saved is a penny earned."*
>
> Or,
>
> **Your Honey:** *"I think I wanna buy a new phone."*
>
> **You:** *"But you just said a penny saved is a penny earned."*
>
> **Your Honey:** *"That was for you. I'm spending my penny."*

Brad says:

> (*A Penny Saved Is A Penny Earned*)

- A penny saved is a waste of a penny. Honestly, what does a penny get you now?
- A penny saved is just another penny stuffed in your car seat cushions or melded with gum and soda at the bottom of your car ash tray.
- A penny saved is one you didn't spend at the strip club and therefore didn't get your ass kicked for spending pennies at a strip club. And that makes a better saying: "A penny saved just saved your ass from being kicked at a strip club!"
- If you consider saving money the same as earning money, then you … well … I don't know …Actually, if you are doing that then you certainly have more money than me and I could learn from you.
- You could spend your hard earned sixth grade allowance on that Indian bead belt at the souvenir shop, or you could save that money and spend it three minutes later on that kick-ass

Indian head-dress over there. A penny saved is a penny earned, indeed!

- Back when I used cash for goods and services, I'd always ask for change, *"Can I get a dollar of that in quarters, please?"* I'd then put those quarters in a jar. I'd do this anytime I paid cash for something. When the jar was full, I'd take it to a bank where they'd run it through their counter for free and deposit it. It was a great way to save money which I later spent on goods and services anyway. Moral of that story? None, no moral. I'm just bragging about my money saving habits and complaining about not having money now. Also, none of those things exist in my life now: I never use cash and I never go to a bank. I think they have machines to count coin now and they charge you coin for counting your coins. Coin or Coins? That word sounds weird now.

A Picture Is Worth A Thousand Words

"Breaking Home Ties" by Norman Rockwell 1954

Explanation:

A single picture of a scene, person, expression, etc. can share the same sentiment that might take a thousand words to describe. Sometimes a picture can 'tell' a story just as well as a thousand words or more. Norman Rockwell's paintings are fine examples.

History:

The origin of this phrase is rife with complications as to who actually started it. It was thought to be Japanese and later Chinese, possibly by Confucius, but all of those were not the true origin. Its roots lie in advertising…

Frederick R. Barnard used the phrase in a 1921 advertisement slogan on the benefit of using pictures on street cars in *"Printer's Ink"* which stated:

"One look is worth a thousand words."

And later, in 1927, old Fred changed it up a bit and used the slogan:

"One picture is worth ten thousand words."

Whoa, now that's inflation! Fred claimed it was "an ancient Chinese proverb" so people would take it more seriously.

Why all this information before I tell you the real truth? Creative freedom. But also to help illustrate how confusing sayings and/or phrases can be as they are bastardized into amalgams of several variants. Social media is certainly more digestible when we can watch a video or picture of cats rather than reading about cats. Society has become incredibly lazy and we'd rather post pictures of our eight-year-olds' birthday party than visit Grandma and tell her the story. But then again, Grandma is probably happier at home with her blue hair and hooch than at your eight-year-old's ankle-biter party.

Ultimately, it is American in origin in the early 1900's and used in the US press quite a bit after that. Arthur Brisbane, of the "Syracuse Advertising Men's Club" gave an instructional talk on journalism and publicity in 1911, where he stated:

"Use a picture. It's worth a thousand words."

Example:

Two patrons standing in an art museum looking at an award winning photograph from that year's war. The photograph shows a dog nuzzling a dying soldier while another man performs CPR; his blood splattered face, fatigued. Just three feet behind them a lone gunman stands with his rifle pointed at their heads looking desperate, scared, and determined.

Both patrons are quiet for some time, taking in the photograph. One of them sheds a tear, hugs the man next to him, and says,

> *"They say a picture is worth a thousand words and I think this picture says them all for me... Thank you for saving my life that day."*

Brad says:

(A Picture Is Worth A Thousand Words)

- Some pictures are worth a thousand dollars. And those pictures are bought by fools.
- I know a woman who spoke 1000 words describing a coupon she had for 24 bars of soap she could buy for $2. I wish I had that time back.
- I dated a girl who thought everything was worth a thousand words because no matter what she looked at, she wouldn't stop talking about it.
- Do you know those pictures that are made up of a thousand smaller pictures? Well, that's a picture that's worth a thousand pictures which means it's worth one million words!
- A picture of the Declaration of Independence is a picture worth 1458 words.

(P.S. – It took 593 words for this entry. I should have just put half of a picture here instead of all the words. What picture you might ask? The back half of a horse).

Piece Of Cake
Easy As Pie
A Cake Walk

Explanation:

All three of these phrases mean the same thing; they describe something that can be easily done. They are used to imply that whatever it is you are about to do is going to be quite easy. If you're fully prepared for a test and have all the confidence in the world, you'd think that test is going to be "as easy as pie" or it'll be a "piece of cake." That test will be "a cake walk".

History:

Piece of cake: American poet Ogden Nash in *"Primrose Path"* in 1936:

> *"Her picture's in the papers now, and life's a piece of cake."*

Easy as pie: "As nice as pie" was close to easy as pie and first used in *"Which: Right or Left?"* By Garrett and Company in 1855:

> *"For nearly a week afterwards, the domestics observed significantly to each other, that Miss Isabella was as 'nice as pie!'"*

A cake walk: Derivative/Variant of piece of cake. It is said that slave owners would throw parties and have their slaves compete in cake walks. Slaves would mock the gestures of the slave owners and best performance would be awarded with a cake.

Example:

> **Rex:** *"We've beaten these guys before AND they've lost their two best players...This game will be as easy as pie."*

> Or,

> **Larry:** *"I don't think I can make it!"*

> **Bob:** *"Sure you can, Larry, you've jumped that far before."*

> **Larry:** *"Yeah, I don't know."*

> **Bob:** *"Come on, it'll be a piece of cake for a guy like you. You can make it!"*

> Or,

> **Bob:** *"I sure feel bad that Larry didn't make that jump."*

> **Cindy:** *"Jumping 20' over a Tiger pit isn't a cake walk, Bob!"*

> **Bob:** *"Is there going to be cake at this wake?"*

Brad says:

> *(Piece Of Cake / Easy As Pie / A Cake Walk)*

> ➤ I've never understood this one, even after doing the research I still don't understand how something is "as easy as pie." Pie isn't easy. Cake isn't easy. You have to purchase ingredients, put those ingredients together in some orderly fashion, apply heat, wait awhile…It's anything BUT easy. You know what's easy? Water. Water is the easiest thing to make. However, if I were to say, "Eating pie is a water walk." That would be

crazy because walking on water is very difficult. Air is pretty much everywhere, except in space, so something like, "Catching slugs is a piece of air," makes complete sense and we'd all be better off using that more often.

- I am probably the only person on the planet that doesn't care for cake. I like pie. Oddly enough though, I do like and eat cupcakes. I'm a complex individual with low self-esteem and the inability to accept that cupcakes are tiny cakes in cup form. I think it's that cupcakes only have the one layer of frosting…The fact that I don't eat cake makes me the most invited person at birthday parties.

- If things were "as easy as pie" why don't we have more pie? I rarely see pie. The same for cake- once a year at your own birthday party and then maybe two more times a year because you only have two friends? And I've done "cake walks" and those aren't easy. I've never won a cake during a cake walk. I've won degradation for pushing children down during a cake walk, but never a cake.

- I'm starting to believe this saying is as dumb as cake.

The Pot Calling the Kettle Black

Explanation:

This phrase is used to criticize someone else for a fault you have yourself.

History:

You pick the date:

1. Shakespeare's *Troilus and Cressida*, in 1606, read:

    "*The raven chides blackness.*"

2. But in Cerantes' Don Quixote in 1620 was translated to:

    "*You are like what is said that the frying-pan said to the kettle, 'Avant, black-browes'.*"

3. And then we have the actual phrase as it is used here by William Penn's *Some Fruits of Solitude* in 1693:

    "*For a covetous man to inveigh against prodigality... is for the pot to call the kettle black.*"

So, the actual phrase was said in 1693 but there are earlier examples of different variations as far back as 1606. It's important you pick a date and defend it well against all your enemies. You don't want to look like the complete idiot that you are... And here I am the pot calling the kettle black. I'm dumber.

Example:

Paul (Carrying a Stolen Television): "*I can't believe Pete called me a liar and a thief.*"

Ken: "*Are you kidding me right now? You're the pot calling the kettle black. Did you get Pete's remote too?*"

Or,

Penny: "*Pamela is so fat this year!*"

Karen (Under Her Breath): "*You're the pot calling the kettle black.*"

Penny: "*What was that?*"

Karen: "*Nothing sweetie. You're right, Pamela is a pig now!*"

Brad says:

(*The Pot Calling the Kettle Black*)

- I think in this case you gotta just go with the talking pot. I mean, it's a *talking* pot for crying out loud! It must be right.
- Even at the cookware level, racism and race baiting is alive and well and needs to stop!
- I'm glad we have more color choices in pots and kettles now, as it makes for a friendlier and inviting kitchen. Not that black pots and kettles make for a less friendlier and non-inviting kitchen. It's just prettier with color. Oh boy, I'm really sinking here. Black is good and color is good. Now, black is really the absence of light so it isn't a color according to physics. On the other hand white is a color when it has ALL the light. Man, even light is racist.
- Why not something like,
    - Look at the lemon calling the banana yellow.
    - Look at the pea calling the pod green.
    - Look at the cracker calling the honky white.

Practice Makes Perfect

Explanation:

The more you practice something, the more you will improve. If you do something frequently, you should be better at it.

History:

It was a proverbial expression as "Use makes mastery" from the mid 1500's, but it is uncertain who said it. But you already knew what this one meant… I just needed some filler so I thought I'd *practice* being simple- that, I'm *perfect* at!

Example:

Sylvester: *"Your daughter is very good on the piano."*

Also Sylvester, But a Different Person (It Can Happen): *"Thank you, she plays all the time and practice makes perfect."*

Brad says:

(*Practice Makes Perfect*)

- Sure, practice makes perfect, unless you've been doing it wrong the whole time.
- *"This is true, because I've been practicing my masturbation for a long time, and I will admit --- I'm perfect at it!"*
- Sometimes you can practice and it doesn't make perfect--- Like farting and pooping; I've been practicing farting my whole life, but every once in a while I'll end up throwing away a good pair of underwear because I was wrong about what was happening.

Quit Cold Turkey

Explanation:

A phrase meaning to quit something immediately without tapering off or slowly reducing whatever it is you are quitting. Usually associated with quitting a drug addiction. To quit cold turkey means you are getting right to the point of never using again.

History:

This idiom most likely stems from the late 1800's term, "talk cold turkey," now shortened to "talk turkey." Talking turkey meant you got right to the point, discussed the issue at hand without any fluff, and always truthful. The variant of this, and the topic we are discussing, quit cold turkey, has the same roots in getting right to the point but mostly used to describe someone quitting drugs.

The earliest reference to drug withdrawal symptoms and cold turkey is from a Canadian newspaper, *The Daily Colonist*, in October 1921:

> "*Perhaps the most pitiful figures who have appeared before Dr. Carleton Simon are those who voluntarily surrender themselves. When they go before him, they [drug addicts] are given what is called the 'cold turkey' treatment.*"

Example:

Man to his cigarette: "*I can't quit you.*"

Cigarette: "*So light me and let's get to it!*"

Man to his cigarette: "*Nope, the best way to quit is cold turkey!*" <Snaps the cigarette in half and tosses the pieces in the garbage.>

Cigarette: "*Ouch.*"

Or,

Cindy: *"I heard your son quit heroin. Good for him!"*

Helga: *"Yeah, but he's still using it every once in a while, we're trying to help him quit gradually."*

Cindy: *"Oh, I thought I read that you needed to quit something like that cold turkey. The success rates are higher than a gradual departure from the addiction."*

Helga: *"That's probably true, but he's also my dealer so that may put a damper in my routine."*

Brad says:

(*Quit Cold Turkey*)

- I quit smoking cold turkey. Mostly because it didn't give me the same high like smoking hot turkey.
- Cold turkey is best turkey.
- There are fewer things less cool than saying, "I just quit heroin cold turkey." Sure, it's a fantastic accomplishment but it seems like a badass sounding drug like "heroin" requires something stronger than cold turkey. Maybe something like:
    - *"I just quit heroin full shark!"*
    - *"I just quit heroin lazer dome."*
    - *"I just quit heroin, slap a monkey!"*

  Ok, apparently, I need to quit heroin.
- Quitting cold turkey cold turkey would be pretty easy.
- Do turkeys bury their heads in the ground when scared? Or are they the ones that drown when they look up? I think they're the drowning bird one, but I also read that was a myth. Ostrich! That's that weird giraffe-bird thing that hides

its head in the sand when scared. Whatever, it just seems people should make tougher references when they are creating idioms, sayings, or phrases. Did the first person say to the second person, "You quit pounding rock like cold turkey?" NO! It was more like, "You quit pounding rock like aggressive dinosaur." I know man and dinosaurs didn't live together. Geez, lighten up, it's just a silly connection. Maybe you should quit heroin cold turkey, too.

➢ I think "talk turkey" came from the first Thanksgiving. All the Pilgrim men were trying to enjoy a meal but all the Pilgrim women were chatting like a field full of turkeys- all kinds of noise but nobody is really saying anything. I think mad Pilgrims decided to kill a turkey and eat it every year to remind them to always keep crazy talking turkey chatter down to a minimum. "Cold turkey" stemmed from that because the only good turkey is a dead turkey and most dead turkeys are cold.

➢ Drug addiction is a serious condition and affects many families across the globe. Get the help you need because your family and friends desperately need you.

- o SAMHSA National Helpline is a free, confidential 24/7, 365 day a year treatment referral and information service: 1.800.662.4357
- o https://www.usa.gov/substance-abuse for information and contact numbers.
- o https://www.help.org/drug-abuse-hotline/ for several different numbers for substance abuse, mental health, suicide prevention
- o Crisis Text Line: text HOME to 741741

Raining Cats And Dogs

Explanation:

This phrase is used to describe large amounts of rain. If it's "raining cats and dogs," it is raining unusually heavy..

History:

Like many of these sayings, raining cats and dogs has a few far-fetched origins. For one, there is no recorded history of cats and dogs raining from the sky. Smaller creatures might get swooped up in heavy winds but a pack of dogs or litter of cats falling from the sky has never been recorded.

The most badass explanation involves the Norse God, Odin. At his side were two wolves and sea captains associated them with rain. Witches were said to take the form of cats and ride the wind! Odin, being the God of many things including storms, would send the wolves (rain) and the cats (wind) to smite those who opposed him.

Finally we have what is probably the actual origin and it's kind of gross: dead cats and dogs would wash down the streets in heavy rains of England in the 18th century. Sure, there would be other garbage washing away but when it rained that much would you notice anything other than the cats and dogs? The reason this is the most likely explanation is because it is the closest to actual and recorded happenings. Jonathan Swift wrote about it in his poem, "*A Description of a City Shower*" in 1710:

> *"...Sweeping from Butchers Stalls, Dung, Guts, and Blood,*
>
> *Drown'd Puppies, stinking Sprats, all drench'd in Mud,*
>
> *Dead Cats and Turnip-Tops come tumbling down the Flood."*

Even before that poem, Richard Brome wrote a comedy called "*The City Wit or The Woman Wears the Breeches*" in 1653 where he used the line loosely connected here:

> *"...and it fhall raine Dogmata Polla Sophon, dogs and polecats, and fo forth."*

It's back when they used 'f' instead of 's' fo you need to tranflate it a bit. Glad they stopped doing that! Polecats are really a weasel but in our lazy speak, it's just easier to drop the "pole" and just shorten to, "dogs and cats."

Personally, I credit the story involving Odin. That happened long before these guys were using modified English to write and speak. Plus, it's a story with witches and wolves and Gods and once again; sea captains. Like I've said before; sea captains are badass' and any story with them in it gets my vote.

Example:

>**Betty:** "*Oh! You're drenched...It must be raining cats and dogs out there!*"

Or,

>**Pat:** "*Ginger, can you believe the flooding after last night's storm?*"

>**Ginger:** "*Don't care-- have you seen Carl the Calico? I let her out yesterday afternoon and haven't seen her.*"

>**Pat:** "*Well, it was raining cats and dogs out there, maybe she met some friends!*"

>**Ginger:** "*Idiot.*"

Brad says:

>(*Raining Cats And Dogs*)

- This would make it easier to rescue pets. Have you tried the pet rescue program? Sheesh, you have to apply, get interviewed, be accepted, pay, and provide a livable home! All that for a puppy you only wanted so you could go to the beach and hit on breezies in their bikinis.
- I'm interested in safety and details... Is it raining Singapuras and Chihuahuas or is it raining Maine Coons and Great Danes? Because one is going to require a hard hat and catcher's mitt and the other will require pickup trucks.
- I've tried many times to make saying, "It's raining cats and dogs out there" sound tough or mean. It just doesn't come across as something a sea captain would say. Maybe these are some things a sea captain might say to describe heavy rain:
  - "*It's raining cannon balls and lead pipe!*"

- *"It's raining asses and tits out there!"*
- *"It's raining ex-wives and girlfriends out there!"*
- *"It's raining wooden legs and hand-hooks!"*
- *"It's raining axes and anvils out there!"*
- *"It's raining cats and ... and ... Are those dogs? I can't tell with this bloody eye patch!*

A Rolling Stone Gathers No Moss

Explanation:

You're not going to like this. Or maybe you will. Sorry, but the explanation for this one is really going to come down to your own personal reflection on whether you think positively or negatively.

There are two sides to this stone and how someone applies it really defines its meaning. The first original meaning has many variants of saying the same thing:

- Someone who is always on the move or cannot settle down, does not have roots in a particular place or in particular people and can therefore never be successful. By constantly being 'on-the-go' they cannot make the time to collect the things that matter in life; friends, prosperity, and love.

The other meaning is essentially the opposite:

- Someone who is always on the move or cannot settle down, does not have roots in a particular place or in particular people and is therefore, more successful. They do not have the burden of obligation or responsibility keeping them from the next big thing that draws them away.

History:

More confusion on the history of another proverb -- Sheesh! Couldn't someone in the sheep fields take better notes back then?

We know for sure it was in use by 1546 when John Heywood's *"A dialogue conteinying the nomber in effect of all the proverbes in the Englishe tongue"* was published. But that is simply a collection of proverbs—just a guy taking the initiative to write stuff down for all of us to enjoy.

Perhaps the most popular history of this proverb is that of the Latin phrase by Erasmus in his collection of Greek and Latin proverbs, "*Adagia*" in 1508. Certainly you've heard of that? But he was just another guy collecting phrases and jotting them down on cocktail napkins—what else would you do during the Renaissance? "*Adagia*" is a collection of thousands of proverbs but that isn't where this proverb came from. And I just told you about that to pad my word count.

Finally, some credit for the origin goes to Publilius Syrus who was a slave but was freed by his master who then educated him in the 1st century BC. It was the original "Running Start" program. He became a writer, actor, and probably an excellent dancer since his work is primarily in Latin – yes, I'm profiling. Why doesn't he receive full credit for the proverb? Because it doesn't appear to be in any of his texts! But he did have a similar sentence in his work, "*Sententia*" (Sentences). That sentence was actually:

> "*People who are always moving, with no roots in one place, avoid responsibilities and cares.*"

So Publius (often printed incorrectly this way, and used here for completeness) gets credit for the origin. Of course in the 1st century BC, those texts were probably written on rocks and we all know rocks are for skipping across ponds. So that probably happened. I wonder if they ever scratched ideas in the moss. We used to do that with cattails! Not real cats, and not real tails – it's a wetland plant. I think I was a lot like Publilius in that we both played with the same technology; sticks, weeds, and flowerless plants.

Example:

Negative Nancy: "*Charlie sure seems to be struggling. Any ideas on what's stopping him from being successful?*"

Negative Ned: *"Well, I'd say he's a rolling stone that gathers no moss as he's always on the go and doesn't have time to build those business relationships."*

Or,

Positive Pam: *"Charlie sure seems successful, what is his strategy?"*

Positive Paul: *"He's always on the go, grabbing that next big idea, and doesn't have anything tying him down. He's a rolling stone that gathers no moss and he's free to explore without the burden of visiting his parents."*
<A single tear rides the groove down Positive Pam's aged face and into the corner of her mouth. Bitter taste. Go see your parents.>

Brad says:

(*A Rolling Stone Gathers No Moss*)

- ➤ This isn't true in the case of a moss covered stone rolling across a patch of moss. That's just moss gathering with friends. We should be like moss.
- ➤ This is true in the case of your own butthole. If you sit too long, the "moss" that grows is called a hemorrhoid.
- ➤ I always thought this was a positive statement because moss is bad, right? As long as you're moving, you won't have any moss growing on you. Moss is bad and we don't want moss on our roofs. It's weird that bad things grow where they shouldn't. Why moss? I can't let that go. Why not, "a rolling stone gathers no roses." That way, if I were stagnant I'd have pretty flowers growing, not ground cover clumps of intertwined nastiness.

- Some stones can't roll. I feel bad for those stones because then moss comes in and moves all over them and makes the stone green and covered in a warm blanket of softness. And the moss has a new stable home. I guess I shouldn't feel bad; this is a win-win.
- I think I've gone insane.
- Stop talking about this one.
- No mas!

Saved By the Bell

Explanation:

This saying refers to being rescued at the last possible moment. Someone who is "saved by the bell" received help right before imminent peril, even death.

History:

This phrase came from the late 1800's from the wonderful sport of boxing; the "I punch your face, you punch my face" world of professional and legal ass-kicking. A fighter was said to have been saved from defeat by the bell that is sounded to end each round. The earliest printed form is from a Massachusetts newspaper titled, *"The Fitchburg Daily Sentinel"* in February of 1893:

> *"Martin Flaherty defeated Bobby Burns in 32 rounds by a complete knockout. Half a dozen times Flaherty was saved by the bell in the earlier rounds."*

That's a 32 round beat down! That must have been a fly weight division rivalry- how could they possibly have gone 32 rounds?

Example:

Boxing Referee: *"...5...6...7...8."* <DING! DING! DING!>

Boxer, Slurring Through a Hole in His Cheek: *"Saved by the bell again. I'm getting good at this!"*

Or,

Brett: <Whispering>*"Carl, you better hurry, there are only 10 minutes left to finish the test!"*

Carl: "*I know, Brett! I'm just not going to finish on…*" <Fire alarm rages throughout the high school.>

Carl, racing towards the exit: "*YES! Saved by the bell!*"

Brad says:

(Saved By the Bell)

- I was saved by a belle, from masturbation.
- Being saved by "Tinkerbell" might be cool because magic! Also, first bullet above. I just killed Disney for myself.
- The Liberty Bell couldn't be saved from a crack in its own bell. No justice for bells, I guess.
- Remember when company would come over to your house and they'd ring the doorbell? That saved me from conversations with my parents.
- Hunger is squelched by the dinner bell.
- Saved from stampeding cattle? Thanks cowbell!
- NOT saved by sleigh bells.
- Happiness saved by jingle bells.
- Sleep ruined by alarm bells.
- Ran over by punk teens? Nope, saved by the hilarious bicycle bell.

Serious As a Heart Attack

Explanation:

This saying is used to emphasize the gravity of your statement or situation, usually in response to the question, "Are you serious?"

History:

This is just a saying or expression, there isn't any concrete history on this one. So, we'll make up our own: Hillbilly One was rattle-canning his pickup when is buddy mosey'd on over and pulled up a hay bale. The two of 'em shot the breeze for a good long time before his cow-tippin' buddy says,

> **Hillbilly Two:** *"Hey there, man. You gonna just rattle can that paint on like that? 'Cause that's pretty sweet right thar."*

> **Hillbilly One:** *"You know it, buddy! I'm dun, done messin' 'round. Tommora, I'm puttin' 40's all 'round, stretch it from here to your shed, slap a 4-banger under da hood, and race this pig, night afta next!"*

> **Hillbilly Two:** *"You serious?"*

> **Hillbilly One:** *"S'rious as a moth-r-funnin heart attack, buddy!"*

I'm sorry, I just finished re-reading, *The Adventures of Huckleberry Finn* by Mark Twain. Bad influence, and honestly, not the best book I've read. Sorry, but I didn't get it. It is hard to write broken speech, I can appreciate that, but I'm as serious as a heart attack; I would not recommend that book!

Example:

> **Dude:** "*So I told her I was only going to pay her $50 for the service, because they didn't finish!*"
>
> **Dude's friend:** "*They didn't even finish the job? Are you serious?*"
>
> **Dude:** "*Serious as a heart attack! I had to finish the job myself!*"

Brad says:

(*Serious As a Heart Attack*)

- ➢ I think a heart attack is a result of some very serious symptoms. "*Serious as having 4-digit cholesterol numbers.*"
- ➢ Sometimes heart attacks aren't that serious but they can get you out of working. Then your family takes care of you like you almost died… Because you did almost die! Still, lying around the house getting paid and fed by other people has a serious appeal --- serious as a heart attack!
- ➢ I saw a guy have a heart attack. He sort of just massaged his own left arm a bit, grimaced, clutched his chest and fell down. It didn't look that serious. He looked sort of dumb. Maybe the idiom should be, "*As dumb looking as having a heart attack.*" I'd use it a lot more than I do now.
- ➢ Maybe it's not the heart attack that is so serious. Perhaps we should address the causes of heart attacks and in particular heart disease. For instance, diet is the largest contributor to heart attacks followed by genetics. Your cholesterol should be checked regularly and a healthy eating habit should be started right now.
- ➢ What just happened? That got all serious, did not expect that turn. Along those lines, saying something is as serious as a

heart attack might be insensitive to someone who has recently had a heart attack (or a loved one for that matter). They might be offended. So, we can choose our words differently as to not offend. Or, we can toughen up like the humans we were meant to be.

A Stitch in Time Saves Nine

Explanation:

Literally, if you fix a hole in fabric early, it can save you from having to fix a larger hole later, thus saving time. One stitch now might save you from having to make nine (or more) stitches later.

Also, in life, if you can deal with something early, it can help prevent bigger problems later on. Think preventative maintenance on your car: routine oil changes now will make your engine last longer and may prevent/delay other costly car problems.

History:

Remember when people used to sew stuff rather than buy a new one from a thrift shop? Me neither, but they did. Well, this English proverb roots to another long titled book by Thomas Fuller in 1732:

"Gnomologia, Adagies and Proverbs, Wise Sentences and Witty Sayings, Ancient and Modern, Foreign and British"

"A stitch in time may save nine."

That's really the title, I can't make this stuff up. I also can't stop thinking it might be a book about Gnomes (Gnomologia) but I read some of it... No gnomes. Just another dude collecting words he hears in a bar or field.

Example:

You, Being Lazy: *"My car brakes seem really squeaky, maybe next month I'll get them checked out."*

Your Dad, Being a Dad: *"I wouldn't wait- if they are bad you risk ruining the rotor and that's even MORE money. A stitch in time saves nine, I'd get your brakes fixed, pronto!"*

Brad says:

(A Stitch in Time Saves Nine)

- ➢ Wearing one condom now can prevent 9 months of "aggressive destructive criticism" along with a lifetime of dependency.
- ➢ Does anybody stitch anymore? I had to look that up and I'm still confused.
- ➢ Misheard lyrics to the unpopular rap tune: "*A Chick On Time, Enjoys My Nine*"
- ➢ The last time I saw a hole in my shirt, I looked at it and said, "*Huh*." Now I continue to wear that same shirt 13 years later. No stitching, no time saving, just a freaking comfortable shirt.
- ➢ I'm not sure where I heard the following but reads like something my grandma would, or did, say:

  > "If you *scuff** your *britches**, I'll *mend** 'em in a *fortnight** at the *sewing bee**."

*Words I've never used until just a minute ago.

Take It with a Grain of Salt

Explanation:

This phrase means to not necessarily accept a statement or story for full fact. Be skeptical of the full meaning of what someone is saying or writing- even me, right now. People may use this phrase as a warning that what they are about to tell you may or may not be true.

History:

Spices tend to make food tastier and/or easier to eat. It would seem most things are easier swallowed with salt. In fact, salt was used as a disinfectant, preservative, even as currency. Sources cite Pliny the Elder in his *"Naturalis Historia,"* in 77 A.D. where he translates an ancient poison antidote which includes the last line of,

> *"...with the addition of a grain of salt; if a person takes this mixture fasting, he will be proof against all poisons for that day."*

However, it was during medieval times that the translation of this saying was created as we use it today. It has been in use since the 17th century attributed to John Trapp's *"Commentary on the Old and New Testaments,"* in 1647:

> *"This is to be taken with a grain of salt."*

Example:

> **Elizabeth:** *"Take this with a grain of salt, but I thought the chicken was horrible."*
>
> **Maribelle:** *"Of course you did, you're a vegan!"*
>
> **Elizabeth:** *"I told you to take it with a grain of salt. I didn't even try it."*
>
> Or,

Chad: *"Jane, I have to take everything with a grain of salt from you."*

Jane: *"Why?"*

Chad: *"Because, you said Sharknado was a great movie series!"*

Jane: *"It IS a great movie series! Would have been better had they killed Tara Reid's character in the third one."*

Brad says:

(Take It with a Grain of Salt)

- I don't add salt to my food, but I do lie. So take everything I say with a grain of salt which includes that statement.
- I think too much salt is bad for your blood pressure. But too much lying about stuff is just going to get your nose punched in. Stop lying and using salt as a crutch.
- I think if you start your statement with, "Take this with a grain of salt, but blah-blah-blah…" it just means you don't know the truth. You're starting out by telling your audience that the next thing you say is going to be a lie and you're going to have to find out if it's true or not. It's an easy way to state non-facts and just hope nobody calls you out on it. Like these examples:
    - *"Take this with a grain of salt, but I'm pretty sure I'm NOT the biggest jerk in the room right now."*
    - *"Take this with a grain of salt; I'm the best ping-pong player you'll ever know."*
    - *"Take this with a grain of salt but size doesn't matter."*

- "Here, take this with a grain of salt." Said the man as he handed his daughter a thimble sized piece of steak. Get it? It's such a tiny piece of meat that it only needs a grain of salt! Bwhahahaha. Explained literal jokes are the best jokes.

There Is More Than One Way to Skin a Cat

Explanation:

This means that there is more than one way to achieve something. A proverb used to describe that problems usually have more than one solution.

History:

Seba Smith wrote *The Money Diggers* in 1840:

"There are more than one way to skin a cat, so are there more ways than one of digging for money."

Other variations of the phrase were:

1678, John Ray's collection of English proverbs
"There are more ways to kill a dog than hanging."

1855, Charles Kingsley in *Westward Ho!*

> *"There are more ways of killing a cat than choking it with cream."*

Still, other uncredited variations were:
> *"There are more ways of killing a cat than by choking it with butter."*

> *"There are more ways of killing a dog than choking him with pudding"*

Example:

Son: *"Dad, these nails just keep splitting the wood!"*

Dad: *"There is more than one way to skin a cat, try using screws. Or, you can pre-drill the holes before nailing. Or you can blunt the tip of the nail to help avoid splitting. Plenty of ways to skin this cat."*

Or,

Daughter: *"How can I make any money mowing lawns? It's raining again!"*

Mother: *"You could have a garage sale. You could go door-to-door offering to clean bathrooms. You could even get baby-sitting jobs for money. There's always more than one way to skin a cat."*

Brad says:

(There Is More Than One Way to Skin a Cat)

- Nope, pretty sure there is just one way to remove skin from a cat.
- …And there is more than one way to rape a dog. But that still doesn't make it right.
- How about, "there are more ways to *pet* a cat?" Stroke, brush, scratch, rub, etc. I don't think people knew what to do with cats back then.
- What was going on in the 1500's-1800's? Skinning cats, curiosity killing cats, they were throwing babies out with bathwater, they ate crow and compared people to 'black sheep.' They even hung birds around their necks, shook lambs tails, and kept their cats in bags. It was not a good time to be an animal, especially a cat!

A Time to Live and a Time to Die

Explanation:

This means something to the effect that we are born, we live and then we die. The title doesn't say it, but it's implied that you should do something with the time in between. We are given two times- one to live and one to die. You can't do anything with the time when you die, so make the most of the time you have to live.

I don't think I've ever heard this one before. Reminds me of the statement regarding the birth and death date of someone's head stone: 1905-1945. It's a start and end date and your life is that dash in between. Do the most you can with your dash.

History:

From the Bible:

> Ecclesiastes 3:1-4. *"A time to be born, and a time to die; a time to plant, and a time to pluck up that which is planted..."*

I keep singing "Turn! Turn! Turn!" By The Byrds.

Example:

Usually used in conjunction with something you or someone else should probably be doing. Someone might be unsure about doing something like taking an important test, or perhaps they don't want to clean their room, you might say:

"There's a time to live and a time to die, might as well get this over with and clean up all your crap. Then you can get back to the living part."

Brad says:

(*A Time to Live and a Time to Die*)

- Hopefully the time to live and time to die aren't real close together.
- I'll take just the time to live, please.
- …And yet I don't have time to wash my socks.
- If someone was going to jump off a bridge and kill themselves, you might tell them, "*Well, there's a time to live and a time to die.*" You of course should never counsel anyone who is attempting to jump off a bridge because you clearly say the wrong things.
- Sometimes, you're at a real boring play or kid function and you wish that the "time to die" part was sooner rather than later. But then you quickly realize that going out for ice cream after this function isn't going to happen for you if you're dead. So you just sit there, slowly dying a little bit with each passing minute. Remember; ice cream!
- It's time to die for this biblical expression.

Two Heads Are Better Than One

Explanation:

Two people thinking about a problem may come to a better solution sooner than one person.

History:

Geez, did anyone other than John Heywood record this stuff? This proverb is from *"A dialogue conteinyng the nomber in effect of all the prouerbes in the Englishe tongue"*, 1546:

> *"Some heades haue taken two headis better then one: But ten heads without wit, I wene as good none."*

That is a direct quote above - that was not me. Sure, I butcher the language and take liberties, but dang I couldn't read that quote twice the same way. Not dissing on Mr. Heywood, shoot, the dude provides a bulk of my work here, but you have to admit you thought I just typed that and left it that way, didn't you?

Example:

Johnny: *"Hey Billy, I couldn't figure it out so I asked Jimmy to help me. He saw the problem and we were able to finish ahead of time. I guess two heads are better than one."*

Billy: *"Or Jimmy's head is better than yours."*

Brad says:

(Two Heads Are Better Than One)

➢ Unless one of your heads is really ugly and has canker sores on its lips, spits when it talks, likes to sing show tunes, and smokes cigarettes. Then a single head would be better.

➢ If one of the heads is trying to solve the problem but the other head keeps saying stupid stuff and makes jokes and otherwise completely distracts both heads from accomplishing anything, then the stupid but funny head guy is getting all the chicks. Boo-yeah! In that case, two heads are better than one; one makes the other look better.

➢ If a person has two heads and two brains, which one controls the functions of the body? Do they both feel pain and say, "*Ouch!*" at the same time? Can one start to walk left and the other brain change direction? Oh! When one brain controls the fart box, can the other shut that sphincter and prevent embarrassment? Does one brain find someone else attractive but the other brain sees me? I have too many questions for two headed folk.

➢ Two heads are better than one for some problems, but not for the problem of deciding which head gets to stay with the body post amputation.

Two Shakes of a Lamb's Tail

Explanation:

This implies that something can be done quickly or with very little effort.

History:

Think of shepherds working the fields and a bunch of little lambs hopping, skipping, and frolicking about. Furry tails and fluffy little bodies bounding to and fro! Pretty cute. Not related to any history of the expression but I'd just like to see that more often in my life.

The full phrase was printed in news articles in the 1840's and advertisements later in the late 1800's and early 1900's, but not credited to anyone in particular.

Scientists, around 1940, needed a term to describe an incredibly short period of time during their research on... Anyone? Anyone? The first atomic bomb! A 'shake' was a unit of time equivalent to 10 nanoseconds.

That's right, the reason Americans aren't speaking Japanese right now is due, in part, to scientists cleverly disguising the time it takes to completely annihilate a city by using a unit of measurement that refers to the tail of a cute, furry, farm animal.

EDIT: I missed this in earlier research but in 1907, Richard Barham is credited with the phrase in his book, *"The Ingoldsby Legends."*

You're welcome.

Example:

>**Anxious Woman:** *"Sir, I need these copies done right away!"*
>
>**Lying Copy Guy:** *"I'll have them done in two shakes of a lamb's tail, mam."*
>
>Or,
>
>< Rarest of conversations; the "customer-happy-with-mechanic" statement: >
>
>**Customer to Another Customer:** *"The repairman said he could fix our tire in two shakes of a lamb's tail, and he was right: we were back on the road in no time."*

Brad says:

(*Two Shakes Of a Lamb's Tail*)

- "*Holy crap! Why are you shaking that lamb's tail? STOP IT! Once was enough!*"
- ...Because if you try to shake the other end, it bites.
- This saying actually spawned the other, more appropriate saying, "*You should never shake a lamb's tail.*"
- Why two shakes of a lamb's tail? ...Because, that's how you greet a lamb.
- Because one shake just isn't satisfactory – for you or the lamb.
- So, there I was standing in a field enjoying the sunset and thoughtfully shaking a lambs' tail. I was content and happy in my own space, unaware of others. The lamb looked back at me, stealing my attention from the ocher horizon as the setting sun blazed away...

    Me: "*Wazzup, lamb?*" I said, comfortably.

    Lamb: "*Baaa-Baaa-Baaaaaa?*" He nodded towards his tail.

    Me: "*I'll stop in two shakes...Oh, I get you.*" I let go.

    The tail slammed down harshly against his butthole and he 'lamb-kicked' me in fright. I clutched my nuts and fell to the ground. The lamb circled my fetal frame and started head butting my back, neck, head, and shoulders.

    Me: "*Stop! Two shakes, two shakes!*"

    The lamb got tired and waddled off. I collected myself, looked around and then scurried home on my unicycle. I'd never stand in a field again and enjoy the gentle shaking of a lamb's tail after that day. Later in life I would find something in my pants way more fun to play with; a fidget spinner. Have you seen those things?!

Up the Creek without a Paddle

Explanation:

Being "up the creek without a paddle" means you are in some kind of trouble without means of getting out of it. If you were in a creek in a boat or raft and didn't have a paddle to guide you safely downstream or to shore, you'd be in dire straits. You would literally be "up the creek without a paddle."

History:

This is slang and one of those phrases that isn't exactly traceable to a specific origin that I could find. John Dos Passos uses the phrase in his *"Adventures of a Young Man"* in 1939:

> *"They left the store ready to cry from worry. It was dark; they had a hard time finding their way through the woods to the place where they'd left the canoe. The mosquitos ate the hides off them. 'Well, we're up shit creek without any paddle'."*

Whoa, language! The takeaway from that is to never find yourself in a shit creek, avoid that type of creek at all costs. However, should you find yourself up the creek without a paddle, you now have this phrase and it's questionable history to discuss with whomever you are about to die with.

Example:

Dude: *"Dude, I have to pass this test and I left all my flash cards at home!"*

Other dude: *"Dude, you're totally up the creek without a paddle."*

Dude: *"Dude?"*

Other Dude: *"Dude!"*

Or,

Stranded Son: *"Dad, I'm on the side of the highway with a flat and no spare tire. Do you have a tire or can you come get me?"*

Deadbeat Dad: *"Why don't you have a spare?"*

Stranded Son: *"Ummm, my friends and I used it as a keg table, it's at Jimmy's."*

Deadbeat Dad: *"Jimmy is a dummy and now you're up the creek without a paddle... I'll be right there as soon as I find one, where are you?"*

Stranded Son: *"Thanks, I'm on the 5 Southbound, just before our exit. Don't need a paddle though, maybe a tire?"*

Brad says:

(*Up the Creek without a Paddle*)

- This is stupid because if you were *up* a creek, then you wouldn't need a paddle to get *down* the creek. You could effectively get down the creek, just not efficiently.
- Assuming you're in a boat or canoe and on a creek, you really should have remembered your paddles, dummy.
- Here's an idea: get out of the creek.
- You don't have to be in a creek to need a paddle. For example, if you were caught in a bear trap and the bear that was supposed to be trapped in that bear trap came by to eat

you, you could use a paddle to defend yourself and give the bear nasty splinters before you give him/her bad indigestion.

- ➤ Sometimes you can be in a tough situation and all seems lost. Then your friend, who is with you and in the same situation says something like, *"Boy, we sure are up the creek without a paddle."* That's a situation where you really could use a paddle to plug that mouth of theirs.

What Goes Around, Comes Around

Explanation:

This saying refers to things returning to what they were after completing, or going through some process. The more common word for it now is, Karma.

Karma is a Hindu and Buddhist term for a person's destiny or fate. What you do or say may come back to you in the future- good or bad. If you treat people poorly, you may be treated poorly as well.

History:

Other than the Buddhist connection with Karma, the origin of this is unknown. There is a biblical reference or summary perhaps of Genesis 29:1-30. I'll leave that for the reader to research. My hands get all 'burny' when I touch that thing.

Example:

Katy: *"Sandy! I can't believe Sheryl just quit choir like that!"*

Sandy: *"Didn't you quit your job in the middle of your shift last year? You just left Sheryl high and dry."*

Katy: *"Yeah, so?"*

Sandy: *"Then how can you be so angry about Sheryl quitting choir tonight? What comes around, goes around, my dear."*

Katy: *"Again, ... So?"*

Brad says:

(*What Goes Around, Comes Around*)

- Merry-Go-Rounds go around and come around.
- I think Boomerang's go around and come around. Well, not when I throw 'em – they call that a 'stick.'
- You get what you give is similar, but in the 2020's it seems you can do just about anything and not have harsh consequences. What goes around keeps going around and I'm sort of waiting for it to come around and do some well-deserved ass kicking on some folks.
- Karma is fun to watch when it's someone else meeting her. Like those dash cam videos of road rage and then the cop lights 'em up! Is it wrong that those make me happy?
- What goes around, comes around; like:
    a. Herpes
    b. Covid-19
    c. Compliments
    d. Sometimes love
    e. Smiles

When the Going Gets Tough, the Tough Get Going

Explanation:

This phrase means that when things get hard for people, the stronger people will keep working while others might give up. You might use this to encourage others to push forward, work harder, stay strong and finish what you started.

History:

Credited to Coach John Thomas of the Green Hornets football team in Texas newspaper, "The Corpus Christi Caller Times" in September 1953:

<during a football team motivational speech.>

"When the going gets tough, the tough gets going."

Example:

Clifford: *"We'll never finish making 1200 candles by end of day at this pace. I need a break."*

Richard: *"Hey Clifford, we can do it. We got two hours, we'll turn the line speed up, let's throw down!!! Remember, when the going gets tough the tough get going. I'm jumping in to help finish. Let's GO!"*

Clifford: *"No."*

Brad says:

(*When the Going Gets Tough, the Tough Get Going*)

➢ If the tough got going in the beginning, then the going should have never gotten tough to begin with. Lazy toughs.

- When the going gets tough, what are the non-toughs doing? Probably most of the work and maybe making things tougher. Toughs and non-toughs need each other.
- When the going gets tough, the tough say they work for Vandalay Industries.
- I remember asking a coach what that meant, *"When the going gets tough, the tough get going!"*
    - **Me:** *"Yeah, what's that mean?"*
    - **Coach:** *"You suck it up, Myers! You push forward when things get hard. Stop sitting there killing the grass!"*
    - **Me:** *"No, I meant what is 'tough'?"*
- "When the going gets tough, Brad goes home."

You Are What You Eat

Explanation:

Eating healthy food makes a body healthy, while the reverse is also true. To be healthy, you need to eat good food. If you are eating junk food, then your body will feel miserable, sluggish, and you'll feel like garbage and someone might say, "You are what you eat." In this case, it was junk and you feel like junk!

History:

Early 1800's by Brillat-Savarin who wrote, in *Physiologie du Gout, ou Meditations de Gastronomie Transcendante, 1826:*

"Tell me what you eat and I will tell you what you are."

Ludwig Andreas Feuerbach wrote an essay titled *Concerning Spiritualism and Materialism in 1863:*

"Man is what he eats."

But the phrase entered the English language in the 1920's and 30's credited to Victor Lindlahr, the creator of the "Catabolic Diet." In 1942, he published *"You Are What You Eat: how to win and keep health with diet."*

Example:

Son: *"Ugh, I feel so sick after eating all those chips."*

Mom: *"Well son, you are what you eat. Why don't you go get an apple or banana?"*

Or,

Me: *"Man, I really feel like eating a big fat ham!"*

Wife: *"You are what you eat."*

Me: *"What?"*

Wife: *"Huh?"*

Me: *"HAM!"*

Brad says:

(*You Are What You Eat*)

- You are what you eat? Is that why my legs and ass look like cottage cheese?
- Sugar and spice and everything nice. Gwen
- Beer and chips and everything fried. Brad
- This:

    Bully, While Pummeling a Kid: *"You're a little pussy!"*

    Kid Getting Pummeled: *"Well, you know what they say…"*

Your Eyes Are Bigger Than Your Stomach

Explanation:

This means you've taken more than you can handle. Your eyes are bigger than your stomach when you take more food than you can really eat. But it's not always related to just food.

You might take on a project vehicle to build into the workhorse you've always wanted but then find out it's more work than you can handle. Your eyes were bigger than your stomach in that you saw a great thing to do but faltered when the amount of time and dedication exceeded your initial expectations. Your dad might have said this to you when you tried to leave the dinner table with broccoli and cottage cheese left on your plate. But we know you were just saving room for pie!

History:

Unsure about this one but research shows that it dates back to the late 1500's; from England where they eat a lot and have bad teeth, just like in America. I couldn't find any relevant history on this, but if we're going back to late medieval times for it, I'd guess a mom said this to her fat king son at some time.

Example:

Big Boned Brad: *"I'm full! I can't eat anymore."*

Skinny Dad: *"Well, you took too much again. I tell you time and time again; your eyes are bigger than your stomach! Finish it."*

Big Boned Brad: *"I'm gonna be sick."*

Skinny Dad: *"Then you'll eat that, too."*

Or,

< Mom and son standing in front of a huge buffet: >

Mom: *"Yes, it's all for us, you can try any of it, but remember that sometimes your eyes are bigger than your stomach. Don't waste food."*

Son: *"Then I'm going to need corrective lenses. I EAT TODAY!"*

Brad says:

(*Your Eyes Are Bigger Than Your Stomach*)

- Someone is telling you that you're a glutton. They don't mean you have big, beautiful, 'stomach-like' eyes.
- Perhaps they are giving you a compliment:

    Mark: *"You are not fat! For crying out loud, your eyes are bigger than your stomach."*

    Marilyn: *"Oh, that's sweet of you!"*

    Mark: *"Huh? Oh- I meant boobs, your boobs are better than your stomach. Ugh, I also meant bigger, not better. Your boobs are definitely bigger than your stomach."*

    Marilyn: *"Stop talking... And my eyes are UP HERE!"*

- "Dude, your eyes are not bigger than your stomach! That's impossible because, HAVE YOU SEEN YOUR STOMACH?"
- If your eyes are bigger than your stomach when making a reference to things you tackle, like goals, dreams, and other achievements, then I'd say you were on a positive path. If you're biting off the perfect amount or less on a given goal, are you really achieving much? Go for all of it, make your eyes on a goal be extremely lofty and strive to achieve that goal. If you fail then you've learned more about yourself. Take it all, eat what you can, keep planning that next meal.

Elvis Has Left the Building

Explanation:

The show is over and it's time to leave. Something has ended, go home.

History:

Among several other famous musical artists of the 1950's who are credited with inventing Rock and Roll music, Elvis Presley was one of them. However, Elvis never claimed to have invented Rock and Roll himself. What he did invent was gyrating hips to music which led to some of your mother's first dry humping's. Sorry, but it's probably true, call her and ask.

The statement, "Elvis has left the building," was announced at the end of Elvis Presley's concerts to encourage fans to leave. It signified the end of the show and that there would be no more encores or stage presence for Elvis. It's used now primarily to mean a sudden end or quick exit.

However, one source cites that the statement was first used to encourage fans to take their seats! Elvis was a regular performer on "The Louisiana Hayride" which was a radio and later television country music show. Elvis was quite popular (see earlier statement about dry humping's) and was on early in the show. The announcer at that time in December of 1956 said;

> *"Please young people, Elvis has left the building. He has gotten in his car and driven away. Please take your seats."*

Example:

Eddie: *"We won the final race!"*

Brett: *"YEAH, Elvis has left the building! Let's pack up and celebrate."*

Or,

Ethan: *"Come on, Eva, let's dance one more time."*

Eva: *"It's late, the food is gone and you drank all my liquor...I believe Elvis has left the building."*

Ethan: *"Who's this Elvis guy?"*

Eva: *"Good night, Ethan."*

Brad says:

(*Elvis Has Left the Building*)

- And with this last idiom/saying/phrase, I too shall leave the building.
- I hope you've enjoyed my 'show' and share with your friends.
- Thank you for supporting and providing me with an outlet to be heard and maybe even laughed at.
- Thanks to my family and friends for the years of laughter.
- Final thanks to my perfect wife for all the joy and dry humping's over the years. You truly are my reason. If I were told I could be happier, I'd never believe it. Although, I haven't tried heroin.
- Don't do drugs, ...Read instead!

References

There are many great resources for finding the etymology of words and phrases. The following list of references were sometimes used to collaborate and compare data to help me form accurate content. Please visit these sites for your etymology needs.

- The Phrase Finder : http://www.phrases.org.uk/index.html
- Wikipedia: http://en.wikipedia.org/wiki/Main_Page
- Historically Speaking: https://idiomation.wordpress.com/a-z-of-entries/
- BookBrowse: https://www.bookbrowse.com/expressions/
- Oxford English Dictionary: https://www.oed.com/
- Book: "*Random House Dictionary of America's Popular Proverbs and Sayings: Second Edition*" by Gregory Titelman

www.ingramcontent.com/pod-product-compliance
Lightning Source LLC
Chambersburg PA
CBHW071525040426
42452CB00008B/888